Japanese Cooking for Gaijin
Make All Your Japanese Favourites At Home!

Elle Kaye

JAPANESE COOKING FOR GAIJIN

Copyright © 2009 - 2021 by Elle Kaye

All rights reserved. No part of this publication may be reproduced, distributed, or transmitted in any form or by any means, including photocopying, recording, or other electronic or mechanical methods, without the prior written permission of the publisher, except in the case of brief quotations embodied in critical reviews and certain other non-commercial uses permitted by copyright law.

ISBN 978-1-990428-04-3

1. Cooking —2. Japanese Cooking — 3. Travel Writing

First Edition

Daruma-San

The Daruma
"Nana korobi ya oki"
"Fall down seven times, get up eight."

This fearsome looking guy is a Daruma. He represents goals, wishes, and achievement. He has a weighted bottom so that if he gets knocked over, he will bounce back.

Darumas come with two blank eyes. Make a wish, write it on him, and fill in one eye. When your wish comes true or you achieve the goal, fill in the other eye. Create your own Daruma with the ones at the end of this book!

Forward

Growing up, when teachers were talking about "the Silk Road" or Marco Polo discovering spices, I was intrigued. I wanted to go to these places, live in the cultures and learn completely new and different ways of life. History and geography teachers had romanticized the rest of the world throughout my school days.

At 23 twenty-three years old, naïve, and suffering from North American egocentrism, I made a quick decision to get on an airplane and head East leaving everything familiar behind for an adventure my soul was screaming for. Friends that I had gone to university with were already living there and as destiny had given me a glimpse of a future I already hated, it might not seem as life-changing to others as it was to me back then. Most of my family had never been on an airplane. We didn't travel as a family like families on television did - I was raised to believe where we lived was all there was. It didn't really hit me that I was embarking on something completely life-altering until I had landed and immediately my adventure began. When I landed at Narita airport I officially became a "Gajin" – an outside, a foreigner or the literal translation – an Alien.

From the moment I landed at Narita airport, everything was the opposite of everything I thought I knew. I remember waking up my first morning in a Tokyo Gaijin house. A Gaijin house is a place where foreign travelers can rent a bed or a room with other foreigners while they travel or find other accommodations. This particular gaijin house was an addition built onto an older building. Our two floors of living space were up five flights of stairs, excruciating for a Canadian spoiled by elevators and escalators.

When I sat up in my bed to see the sun beginning to rise over what the biggest city in the world at the time, there was seemed to be a dome of haze, like this city was sitting inside a bubble. I remember my jet-lagged brain thinking how sci-fi it appeared and that I was about to realize how much of an "alien" I really was.

Finding jobs teaching English was easy in those days, anyone could get off a plane with their backpack and get work teaching. I soon found work with a large company that had all of us teachers taking trains to schools in remote towns outside of Tokyo. This was the best experience of all. Japan was pure magic to me. Walking the tiny streets that zig- zagged insensibly to the subway, I knew that if I died at any time, I died living life and knowing I had broken out of my own bubble and that made everything all the more exciting!

I lived and worked in Tokyo and Urayasu, Chiba near Tokyo Disneyland. From the 12th-floor balcony of the apartment I could watch the fireworks every night until Emperor Hirohito died and Japan went into mourning! The company I worked for had me working at the school's different locations six days a week meaning I took trains and buses to all sorts of out of the way places in the area. It was exciting and draining and I fell in love with each and every one of my students from the 18-month-old babies to the 80-year-old elders who had incredible stories to tell. Everything was so different, every day was a learning experience, one year wasn't nearly enough and, after a year and a half in Tokyo, I moved to a little city near Mt. Fuji called Numazu.

Numazu is an incredible city. It's small enough to know the community, big enough to offer all kinds of interesting things to do. Again, I feel in love with the people I was teaching and meeting. I had an apartment of my own where on clear days I would pull back the curtains on my window in and have a glorious view of Mt. Fuji like my own person framed picture that changed throughout the day!

Every day was a new adventure in my life in Japan. I loved waiting for the subway trains. I remember standing waiting for the Shinkansen one day – the "bullet train" and

fastest train in the world. There I was in one of the most technologically advanced countries in the world, waiting on a platform with a Sumo wrestler his oiled ponytail pinned up, his huge girth wrapped in a Yukata; on my right and a beautiful older woman in a black kimono, exquisitely detail with embroidery, her grey hair beautifully coiffed, her tiny feet in Geta sandals. Thousands of years of history surrounded me while I waited for twentieth century transportation. My time in

Japan provided me with surreal experiences every day and I loved it.

This book is dedicated to the thousands of students and people in Japan that I was blessed to have met while I lived there. I have wonderful memories of beautiful, funny people that I think about often and wonder how their lives are this many years later. It was my honour to know each and every student as well as all of the folks I met on a day-to-day basis - the lovely owner of the patisserie across from where we lived who had a beautiful grandbaby (that grandbaby probably has children of her own now); the friendly ticket men at the train stations (who patiently listened to my Japanese as I acquired it and replied to me in "Japanglish" to me to help me get where I needed to go); Moms teaching their babies how to bow to say hello to me when I caught their babies staring at the blonde, blue-eyed stranger on buses or subways; tiny old women, wizened from the sun, bent over with the weight of Bamboo boxes of leaves they'd just picked during the day, smiling and bowing hello on local trains.

Part of the joy of teaching and living in Japan is being on the receiving end of unimaginable hospitality. I was often taken places after evening classes and on weekends. Sometimes a need to speak English with other Gaijin took me to flashy Tokyo clubs (where, for $50.00 we stay from midnight 'til the first trains to take us home at 5 a.m. $50.00 got us great music and unlimited food and drink all night!) There was always a McDonalds or Kentucky Fried Chicken to fall back on for Western food cravings, but Japanese food was so incredible, falling back on our North American fast food was rare.

I learned my Japanese flavours by going to my favourite Japanese pubs (Izakaya) where they serve small dishes of amazing traditional Japanese food. I knew that when I left Japan I would really miss Japanese food and although I still miss the atmosphere of a genuine outdoor yakitoria, my recipes bring back familiar tastes that I grew to love. My best memories are tied into the recipes that are in this book. The flavours bring back memories of favourite restaurants, events, parties and being invited to homes for meals. I'm grateful for these memories and treasure the kindnesses that were extended to me. I learned about cooking Japanese food through these opportunities – teaching groups of Japanese housewives, or private lessons with women who wanted to learn English by translating the recipes to English where I would try them on my own and later use them for my family. These are the recipes I have used or adapted over the years so that I can have authentic tasting Japanese food at home.

Perhaps most importantly, I'd also like to give an eternal thank you to Ad and Kelly; without their help I would never be where I am now. While our lives have gone in different directions, I am eternally grateful to them both.

If you have a chance to visit Japan, I urge you to go – you will love the wonderful people, the beautiful country and delicious the food. Have fun with these recipes - I hope you love them as much as my family does!

Table of Contents

Daruma-San 3

Forward 4

Cooking in Japan 14

Japanese Ingredients 15

SOUP 16

    Primary Stock 18

    Secondary Stock 18

    Dried Anchovy Stock 19

    Dried Kelp Soup Base 19

    Mushroom Soup Base 19

    Clear Soup 20

    Classic Miso Soup 21

    Pork Miso Soup 21

    Clear Clam Soup 22

    Japanese Squash Soup 22

    Monk's Vegan Soup 23

    Rice & Grilled Salmon Soup 24

    Chicken and Rice Soup 24

    Radish & Rice Soup 25

    Oyster & Rice Soup 25

PICKLES 26

    Rice Bran 28

    Pickled Vegetables in Nuka 29

    Miso & Rice Bran Pickles 29

    Garlic Pickled in Miso 30

    Pickled Garlic in Soy Sauce 30

    Pickled Daikon Radish 30

    Salted Eggplant 31

    Salted Cabbage & Carrots 31

RICE DISHES 32

    Stove-top Cooked White Rice 33

    Teriyaki Beef Bowl 34

    Teriyaki Chicken Bowl 35

    Beef Bowl 36

    Chicken and Egg "Family Bowl" 36

    Deep-Fried Pork Bowl 37

    Raw Fish Bowl 37

    Tempura Bowl 38

    Mixed Rice Bowl 39

    Rice Balls 40

    Salted Sesame Seed Furikake 41

    Daikon Leaf, Dried Fish and Dried Shrimp 41

    Salmon Flakes 42

    Dried Seaweed and Egg 42

    Bacon Furikake 43

    Grilled Rice Balls 43

    Green Tea and Pickles on Rice 43

SIMPLE SUSHI 44

    Stove-Top Sushi Rice 45

    Rolled Sweet Egg 46

    Sweet Sushi Shrimp 47

    Tofu Pouches 47

    Cucumber Roll 47

    Tuna Roll 48

    California Roll 48

    Nigiri-Sushi 49

    Sushi Cones 50

    Cucumber 50

    Sweet Egg Maki 51

    Pickled Daikon Maki 51

    Spicy Tuna 51

    Spicy Salmon 51

- Spicy Scallop 51
- California 52
- Scattered Sushi Bowl 53

SALADS & DRESSINGS 54

- Green Salad 55
- Seared Beef Salad 56
- Citrus-Soy Salad Dressing 56
- Japanese Potato Salad 57
- Quick Side Salad 57
- Tofu, Ham, and Cucumber Salad 57
- Japanese Noodles with Vinegar Dressing 58
- Miso Salad Dressing 58
- Ginger Salad Dressing 58
- Vinegar Dressing 1 59
- Vinegar Dressing 2 59

SIDE DISHES 60

- Nikujaga 61
- Salted Soybean Pods 61
- Deep-Fried Potato Patties 62
- Bacon-Asparagus Rolls 63
- Broiled Stuffed Japanese Green Peppers 63
- Pan Fried Ham & Onion Wraps 64
- Deep-Fried Natto 64
- Sesame Beef & Green Beans 65
- Braised Burdock Root & Carrots 65
- Pan-Fried Dumplings 66
- Spring Rolls 67
- Chicken and Cheese Spring Rolls 68
- Fried Potatoes and Bacon 69
- Deep Fried Beef with Cheese 69
- Green Beans with Miso 70
- Boiled Japanese Squash 70
- Baked Eggplant with Miso 70

Japanese Pancakes	71

MEAT DISHES 72

Deep-Fried Pork Cutlets	73
Deep-Fried Chicken Cutlets	73
Pork Spareribs and Radish	74
Grilled Chicken on Skewers	74
Deep Fried Pork Skewers	75
Chicken Balls	75
Chicken Wings	76
Fried Chicken and Fries Basket	76
Ground Beef & Vegetables with Cheese	77
Japanese Hamburger Patties	77
Deep Fried Pork Balls	78
Pork Cutlets and Curry	79
Curry Roux Recipe	80

HOT POTS 81

Sukiyaki	82
Beef and Vegetable Hotpot	83
Mixed Stew	84
Tofu Hotpot	85
Miso Layer Hotpot	86
Shabu-Shabu	87
Salmon Miso Hot Pot	88
Chicken Stew	89
Sumo Wrestler's Stew	90

FISH 91

Broiled Clams	92
Easy Salted Salmon	92
Simmered Mackerel	93
Teriyaki Salmon	93
Salted Broiled Horse Makerel	94
Baked Flounder	94
Broiled White Fish	95

- Miso-Marinated Broiled Tuna ... 95
- Braised Flounder with Grated Daikon ... 96
- Crab and Rice Porridge ... 96

EGGS ... 97

- Steamed Egg Custard ... 98
- Hot Spring Eggs ... 99
- Japanese Soft-Boiled Eggs ... 99
- Basic Sweet Rolled Eggs ... 100
- Basic Rolled Eggs ... 100
- Egg Threads ... 101
- Scrambled Eggs with Spinach ... 101

TOFU DISHES ... 102

- Deep fried Tofu in Broth ... 103
- Steamed Tofu Custard ... 104
- Tofu Steak ... 105
- Spicy Tofu ... 106
- Tofu Crab Cakes ... 107
- Chicken Tofu Patties ... 108
- Anchovy Peanut Tofu ... 109
- Okara and Vegetable Sauté ... 109
- Simple Cold Tofu ... 110
- Tofu Fritters ... 110

NOODLES ... 111

- Treasure-Chest Udon ... 113
- Cold Soba Noodles and Dipping Sauce ... 114
- Cold Chinese Noodles ... 114
- Full-Moon Soba ... 115
- Tempura with Noodles ... 115
- Hot Noodles and Chicken in Broth ... 116
- Pan-fried Ramen Noodles ... 117
- Soy Sauce & Butter Ramen ... 118
- Corn Butter Ramen ... 119
- Miso Ramen ... 120

- Ramen Burger 121

DESSERT **122**
- Japanese Strawberry Shortcake 123
- Japanese Parfait 124
- Mochi 124
- Japanese Cheesecake 125
- Mitarashi Dango 126
- Japanese Coffee Jelly 127
- Castella Cake 127
- No-Bake Green Tea Mousse Cheesecake 128
- How to Plan a Japanese Meal 129
- Using Leftovers - How to Make a Bento Lunch Box 129
- YOUR DARUMA FOR SUCCESS - MAKE A WISH! 130

Cooking in Japan

Japanese cooking is simple once you try making a dish. Making it in true Japanese style is the difficult part – aesthetics are as important as the meals themselves. It never failed to amaze me how beautiful Japanese food was, even lunchbox bentos in the convenience store Styrofoam plates were pretty. Life was a gastronomical education in Japan and I quickly became an avid learner.

I learned that Japanese meals are composed of rice, a soup, a salad, pickles, a main dish and two side dishes. The main dish, Rice and soup would be served individually but the pickles and side dishes were communal. The dishes will typically have five colours – red, white, green, yellow, and black, partly for esthetics, partly for nutritional value. Even simple bento boxes at a convenience store will include all these colours in their choice of food they include.

Two-burner counter-top gas stoves with a pull-out broiling grills are typical as opposed to our huge range ovens here in North America. I was amazed that the variety of delicious food was cooked on only two burners and then plated so beautifully. I learned to use chopsticks quickly because they're rarely on a table. I sat on Tatami-matted floors sharing meals at small, square kotatsu family tables….and I loved it.

Before a meal it's traditional to say a sort of "blessing" for the food "Itadakimasu" (roughly translated to "I gratefully partake), whether at home or in a restaurant. After the meal is finished, another traditional phrase "Gochiso sama deshita" ("I have eaten well") shows the cook or host gratitude. When at someone's home, it's polite to comment on the beauty of the dish or how wonderful it smells.

All my recipes are for "San-nin Bun" - for 3 people. Increase ingredient amounts as you need for the number of people you're serving.

Japanese Ingredients

Whether you're dining in a restaurant or a guest in someone's home, in Japanese cooking the rule is "the freshest ingredients the best." Very few parts of a meal are bottled, canned or pre-packaged except for spices or flavour enhancements. You can find the ingredients in Asian food markets and in many larger grocery stores in the international food section. From experience I've learned that using Japanese ingredients for Japanese cooking gets the best results and the least complaints.

Miso comes in light and dark colours and they're used to emphasize different flavours in cooking. Kome Miso is made from soybeans and white rice. Shiro Miso (White Miso) is lighter coloured, Aka Miso (Red Miso) is darker in colour. Another kind of Miso is Mugi Miso which is made from soybeans and barley; it has an intense flavour. Different regions in Japan use different kinds of Miso in their cooking adding to the vast styles of cooking from north to south.

Soy Sauce is also made from soybeans and has various colours and intensity. The darker the Soy Sauce, the saltier it is.

Sake (Rice wine or cooking spirits) and Mirin are both used in Japanese cooking. For real authentic taste, splurging for a bottle of real Sake at a liquor store is preferred, but Asian food markets sell cooking-grade Rice wine. Mirin is a form of cooking sake that is sweetened; sometimes recipes will call for both. They each add a different depth to the flavour of dishes and it's best to use them as they're called for in a dish, do not skimp or substitute.

There are other bottled sauces and dressings mentioned that go with the dishes specifically like Tonkatsu sauce and Okonomiyaki sauce. Some soup bases also come in bottles because the preparation is time consuming, like Soba Mentsuyu. I'll tell you more about these as they're used in each recipe.

I don't use iodized salt in any of my cooking. I find seasalt lends a more authentic taste and is healthier, but recently I discovered Himalayan pink salt which contains 87 minerals that have been removed in the refining of normal table salt. Himalayan pink salt is healthier, tastes the same as any other Salt and I buy it at my local health food store. As with the more natural salt, I prefer organic vegetables and fruit for my dishes when I can get it.

SOUP

SOUP

The centre of Japanese home-style cooking is soup; it's served with almost every meal in the home starting with breakfast. Miso soup is hearty and the soup bases for noodle dishes make my mouth water just thinking about them. Deep, fragrant, delicious, Japanese soup is healthy and delicious. Different areas of Japan each have distinct flavours. As with all my cooking, I'm partial to Tokyo area flavours.

Basically there are two kinds of soup that are served with Japanese home-style meals. One is the ever-famous "Miso-shiru" soup made from Miso (soybean paste). The other is a clear, consommé- type soup called "Sumashi-jiru".

The make or break component of a genuinely great soup (whether it's Miso or Ramen soup) is the soup stock itself, calls "Dashi". Japanese soup stock is made from dried Kombu (Kelp), Katsuoboshi (dried fish flakes) or Niboshi (tiny dried fish). It's times consuming on a daily basis to make Dashi-stock, personally I was never able to understand how housewives were able to make all the wonderful meals and incredible, intricate bento lunch boxes for their kids and husband. Powdered Dashi no moto (fish-based soup stock) is as much of a modern-day miracle as the Shinkansen bullet train in my mind. It also comes in liquid and bag style but I stick with the powdered form. When I'm making a special meal, I'll make this traditional style soup base and store the different soups in glass mason jars.

Primary Stock
(Ichiban Dashi)

Time: Approximately an hour

Kombu (dried Kelp, it comes in a package)
1 cup Katsuoboshi (dried fish flakes)
4.5 cups cold, fresh water

Secondary Stock
(Niban-Dashi)

2 cups cold, fresh water

Step 1

Ichiban Dashi
This can be used for the clear "Sumashi jIru" or Miso soup.

1. Take a piece of Kombu out of the package, use a damp paper towel to wipe off the White powdery film from each side.
2. Use kitchen scissors (the ones you only use in cooking) or a knife to slice the Kombu into 3 inch pieces.
3. Pour water into a stock pan and soak the Kombu pieces in it for 10 minutes.
4. Heat water and Kelp to just before the boiling point, remove the Kelp with a slotted spoon and set aside – it'll be used again.
5. Add the katsuoboshi. Let this simmer for about a minute and a half and then turn the heat off completely. Let the katsuoboshi settle to the bottom.
6. When all of the katsuoboshi have settled on the bottom of the pan, strain the liquid in a steel strainer lined with cheesecloth or paper towel so that the strained liquid is free of katsuoboshi and Kombu.

*Keep the boiled katsuoboshi for the next step

Step 2

Niban Dashi
(Cooking stock for vegetables)

7. Pour 2 cups of water into a stock pan
8. Add the boiled Kombu and katsuoboshi from the first round
9. Bring to a boil and then simmer for 5 minutes
10. Turn off heat and cool for 15 minutes
11. Strain the liquid in a steel strainer lined with cheesecloth or paper towel so that the strained liquid is free of katsuoboshi and Kombu.

Dried Anchovy Stock
(Niboshi Dashi)

This is the traditional soup base for hearty Miso soups. The flavour of this stock is unbeatable.

1 10-inch strip of Kombu (dried Kelp)
2 cups Niboshi (small dried anchovies)
4 cups cold, fresh water

1. Tear off the heads and underbellies off the Niboshi and discard.
2. Wipe the White, powdery film off the kombu
3. Use kitchen scissors (the ones you only use in cooking) or a knife to slice the Kombu into 3 inch pieces
4. Pour 4.5 cups of water into stock pan, add the Niboshi and kombu.
5. Bring the water to a boil, turn heat down to simmer and remove Kelp with a slotted spoon
6. Simmer for 20 minutes, and then turn off heat
7. Let Niboshi settle to the bottom
8. Strain the liquid in a steel strainer lined with cheesecloth or paper towel so that the strained liquid is free of Niboshi and Kombu

Dried Kelp Soup Base
(Kombu Dashi)

3 x 10-inch pieces Dried Kelp (Kombu)
6 cups of water

1. In deep saucepan, soak Kombu in water for 2 hours
2. Bring water and kombu to boil; remove from heat and cool to room temperature
3. Remove kombu (discard)
4. Pour liquid through cheesecloth-lined strainer

Can be stored in refrigerator up to 1 week

Mushroom Soup Base
(Shiitake Jiru)

1 cup dried Shiitake Mushrooms
6 cups of water

1. In deep saucepan, soak shiitake mushrooms in water for 2 hours
2. Bring water shiitake mushrooms to boil; remove from heat and cool to room temperature
3. Remove shiitake mushrooms
4. Pour liquid through cheesecloth-lined strainer

Can be stored in refrigerator up to 1 week

Clear Soup
(Sumashi-Jiru)

3 cups Ichiban Dashi
1 tsp Seasalt (Umi Shio)
½ tsp Soy Sauce (Shoyu)
¼ lb Chicken fillets (Tori Sasami)
¼ tsp Seasalt (Umi Shio) 1 tsp Sake
1 tbsp Potato Starch (Katakuriko) or Cornstarch
3 Shiitake Mushrooms (fresh or dried & rehydrated in water) 8 Snow peas

1. Remove the white tendon from the chicken fillets; cut into 2 inchpieces
2. Season the chicken pieces with seasalt and sake
3. Coat chicken with potato starch (or cornstarch)
4. Remove stems from shiitake mushrooms
5. Cut an "X" (criss-cross) on the top of each mushrooms
6. Trim the snow peas but snapping the top bit off and the thin thread along edges
7. Heat 2 cups of water saucepan
8. Boil chicken for 3 minutes; remove with a slotted spoon and drain
9. Add snow peas for 30 seconds; blanch
10. Remove with slotted spoon
11. Heat pre-made Ichiban Dashi
12. Add tsp seasalt & ½ tsp soy sauce (Shoyu)
13. Bring to boil
14. Divide chicken, mushrooms and snow peas among 3 individual soup bowls
15. Pour hot soup over each bowl

Other ingredients that can be substituted:

Tofu – soft Tofu patted dry with paper towel and cut into half-inchcubes
Shrimp (Ebi) -- deveined and boiled in salted water
Spinach – (Horenso) blanched, water and chopped into 2 inch pieces
Spring onions - (Negi) washed and cut into fine rounds no larger than 1/8 -- inch
Onion – (Tamanegi) peeled and Sliced into paper-thin rounds
Carrot – (Ninjin) peeled and chopped into ¼ inch rounds, added to soup and boiled until soft
Egg – (Tamago) freshly cracked, scrambled, and added to the Dashi at boiling stage
Trefoil – (Mitsuba) laid on the bottom of the bowl to have hot soup poured on it

Classic Miso Soup
(Miso Jiru)

3 cups Ichiban Dashi 4 tbsp Miso paste
1 block soft Tofu
1 Spring onions (Negi)

1. Drain the water from the tofu and place the tofu between two pieces of paper towel on a plate to drain the excess water from the Tofu; set aside 15 minutes
2. Slice the tofu horizontally (9 o'clock to 3 o'clock direction) in half, then vertically lengthwise; continue cutting tofu into ½ inch cubes (12 o'clock to 6 o'clock direction)
3. Slice spring onion into 1/8 inch rounds
4. Heat Ichiban Dashi in a stock pan to low boiling point.
5. Place miso in a ladle and lower into low-boiling Dashi; using a spoon with the other hand, dissolve the miso in the Dashi
6. Add tofu and spring onions; turn down to simmer
7. Ladle gently into individual soup bowls.

Other ingredients that can be substituted:
Dried Seaweed (Wakame) – rehydrated in warm water and chopped into 2 inch pieces Spinach – (Horenso) blanched, water squeezed out and chopped into 2 inch pieces
Onion (Tamanegi) -- Sliced into paper-thin rounds
White Radish – (Daikon) peeled, cut lengthwise into 2-inch slivers remembering to skim the foam (Aku) from the soup as it boils to cook the Daikon
Deep-fried Tofu slices (Aburaage) boiled in water for 1 minute to take off the excess oil. Squeeze out excess oil after going, pat dry and slice into 1/8 inch strips

Pork Miso Soup
(Buta Jiru)

3 cups of Ichiban Dashi
¼ lb. thinly Sliced pork
¼ cup Daikon radish
¼ cup Carrot (Ninjin)
3 taro root or small sweet Potatoes
½ block Konnyaku
¼ cup Burdock Root
2 tbsp Spring Onion (Negi)
1 tbsp Miso

1. Peel and chop daikon radish into 1-inch cubes
2. Peel and chop carrot into ½-inch chunks
3. Peel & halve taros; soak in cold water
4. Wash spring onions and pat dry with paper towel; chop finely
5. Peel burdock root and julienne into matchsticks; soak in cold water with ½ tsp white vinegar
6. Cut konnyaku into 1/8-inch slices; boil in water for 3 minutes and drain; set aside
7. Heat Dashi to boiling
8. Add sliced pork, daikon, carrot, taros (or sweet potatoes), konnyaku and burdock root
9. Boil until vegetables are cooked thoroughly; skim off any foam (aku) that forms
10. Add miso to ladle and lower into low boiling soup; dissolve by stirring with a spoon or ladle
11. Ladle into small, individual bowls

Clear Clam Soup
(Hamaguri Ushiojiru)

3 cups of Niban Dashi
½ lb Baby Clams,
 OR 12-16 small Hamaguri (hard-shell Clams),
OR 3 large Hamaguri
1 tbsp Sake
1 tsp Soy Sauce (Shoyu)
½ tsp Seasalt

Garnish
1 bunch of Nanohana (rape flower), boiled, or Mitsuba (wild Parsley) leaves

1. Scrub clams in water to clean; soak in salted water to extract any shell sand
2. Put Niban Dashi (or water & Dashi no moto and clams in a stock pan)
3. Heat on high and simmer until clams open
4. Remove the clam from the pan and strain the soup with mesh strainer lined with cheesecloth or paper towel to remove grit; save stock
5. Return soup back in the pan and season with sake, soy sauce, and seasalt
6. Divide baby clams, 3-4 small clams or 1 large clam in each small, individual soup bowl
7. Pour steaming hot soup over clams
8. Garnish with boiled nanohana or mitsuba leaves

Japanese Squash Soup
(Kabocha Supu)

1 cup Chicken stock
1 lb Kabocha squash, seeds removed
½ Onion (Negi)
1 Tbsp Butter
1 2/3 cup half and half cream
Seasalt/ Pepper to taste ½ Onion (Negi)
1 Tbsp Butter
1 2/3 cup half and half cream
Seasalt/ Pepper to taste

1. Heat oven to 350°F
2. Peel and slice onions thinly
3. Slice kabocha squash into halve; remove seed cut
4. Bake until tender; cool
5. Scoop flesh from skin; set aside
6. Over medium heat; sauté onion slices with butter in skillet until translucent
7. Add kabocha; sauté together for 3 minutes stirring constantly
8. Add water and chicken stock
9. Simmer on low heat for 30 minutes
10. Remove from heat; let cool
11. Puree mixture in blender
12. Return pureed mixture to pan
13. Add half and half cream; bring to a boil, stirring constantly
14. Remove from heat
15. Season with seasalt (Umi Shio) and pepper
16. Ladle into small, individual bowls; serve hot

Monk's Vegan Soup
(Kenchin-Jiru)

3 cups Niban Dashi
3 inches burdock root (Gobo)
¼ medium Carrot (Ninjin)
¼ lb Daikon radish
1 large White Potato (Imo)
½ Chikuwa (Fish Cake Roll)
½ block Soft Tofu
4 inches Spring onions (Naga-Negi)
2 tsp Sesame Oil (Goma Abura)
2 tsp Soy Sauce (Shoyu)
½ tsp Seasalt

1. Wash spring onions, pat dry with paper towel, slice off root tips (discard) and slice thinly
2. Peel or scrape skin off burdock root and julienne into matchsticks
3. Soak julienned burdock in 1 cup of water with ½ teaspoon of vinegar for 5 minutes; drain, pat dry with paper towel
4. Peel carrot; cut into ½ inch chunks
5. Peel daikon; cut into ½ inch quarter-rounds
6. Peel potato cut into ½ inch chunks
7. Slice chikuwa into thin rounds
8. Heat sesame oil in a stock pot; sauté daikon, gobo, carrot, potato, and chikuwa on medium heat one minute
9. Slice the tofu horizontally (9 o'clock to 3 o'clock direction) in half, then vertically lengthwise; continue cutting tofu into ½ inch cubes (12 o'clock to 6 o'clock direction)
10. Add Dashi soup stock in the pot and bring to a boil
11. Turn down the heat to low and skim off any foam (Aku) that rises to the surface; simmer until vegetables are softened
12. Season the soup with soy sauce and seasalt
13. Add cubed tofu gently to soup, simmer for a minute.
14. Add spring onions (Negi) to soup
15. Turn off heat; ladle into small individual bowls

Rice & Grilled Salmon Soup
(Sake Zosui)

1 ½ cups Cooked Rice
3 cups Ichiban Dashi
3 small pieces Salted Salmon fillet (Shiozake)
3 tsp Sake
1 ½ tsp Soy Sauce (Shoyu)

1. In soup pot (or large, lidded ceramic soup pot), heat Dashi to boiling
2. Cut salmon into bite-sized pieces
3. Add salmon to boiling dash, cook until pink
4. Lower heat to medium, add rice, soy sauce and sake
5. Cover and simmer for 5 minutes, stirring occasionally
6. Serve in individual bowls

Chicken and Rice Soup
(Tori Zosui)

1 ¼ - 1 ½ cups Cooked Rice
3 cups Chicken Stock
1 tbsp Soy Sauce (Shoyu)
6-inch length dried Kelp (Kombu)
1/8 teaspoon coarsely ground black Pepper
½ lb cooked Chicken (skin and bones removed)
1 tsp freshly fresh Ginger root (Shoga)
3 Spring onions (Negi)
Salt and Pepper to taste

1. Peel and grate ginger root; set aside
2. Wash, pat dry and finely slice spring onions
3. Shred chicken into thin strips about ¼ inchwide x 1 ½ -- inches long
4. Put chicken stock and kombu in a large saucepan; let the kombu soak for 10 to 15 minutes
5. Bring stock to a boil over high heat; remove kombu and discard
6. Turn down heat to low; add soy sauce and black pepper
7. Simmer 30 minutes
8. Add rice to stock; simmer over low heat for 15 minutes
   Cooked Rice grains will have doubled in size
9. Add chicken strips and grated ginger simmering Rice soup; stir
10. Remove from heat and let sit 5 minutes, covered
11. Season to taste with salt and pepper
12. Serve immediately in deep bowls; garnish with sliced spring onions

Radish & Rice Soup
(Daikon Zosui)

3 cups Cooked Rice
¾ cup Shiitake Mushrooms, thinly Sliced
1½ cups Daikon radish, sliced (about a four inch-long chunk)
¼ cup Carrots (Ninjin), sliced as directed
½ cup dried Seaweed (Wakame) 6 cups Ichiban Dashi
½ tsp seasalt
2½ tbsps Soy Sauce (Shoyu)

1. Peel daikon; slice thinly into strips 2 inches x ½ inchwide (1/8-inch thick)
2. Peel carrot slice thinly into strips 2 inches x ½ inchwide (1/8-inch thick)
3. Remove stems from shiitake mushrooms and slice thinly
4. Add dried seaweed to ½ cup water to rehydrate; soak 5 minutes
5. Drain re-hydrated seaweed, squeezing out excess water; chop into 1-inch pieces
6. Heat Dashi in deep saucepan over medium-high heat
7. Add daikon and carrots; bring to boil
8. Cook until the vegetables have softened (about 15 minutes)
9. Add cooked rice, mushrooms and wakame; stir; bring to a boil again
10. Remove from heat; stir in salt and soy sauce; let sit covered 5 minutes

Oyster & Rice Soup
(Kaki Zosui)

2 cups Cooked Rice
3 cups Ichiban Dashi
12 freshly shucked oysters (Reserve liquid)
½ tsp Salt
3 tbsps Soy Sauce (Shoyu)
3 tsp grated Daikon radish

1. In medium glass bowl, sprinkle oysters with ½ tsp salt; mix gently to coat oysters
2. Rinse oysters under cold running water to remove sand and salt; pat dry with paper towels
3. In into deep saucepan bring Dashi and reserved oyster liquid to boil over high heat
4. Reduce the heat to maintain a steady simmer, skimming off any foam (Aku) (about 10 minutes)
5. Add rice, stirring gently until lumps are broken
6. Add oysters; cook 1 minute
7. Add soy sauce, stir to distribute well; cook 2 more minutes
8. Ladle into deep bowls, top with 1 tsp grated daikon, serve immediately

PICKLES

PICKLES

Fermented Pickles

These are my personal favorite Japanese pickles, very homestyle and organic. The initial fermentation process is a bit time consuming but once it's finished, it can last for years if it's taken care of well. The housewives I taught in Japan told me that some families have fermented Nuka base that would rate as "antique" with age. I was told that keeping metal away and stirring "by hand" is the traditional way, I use a large wooden spoon though.

It's important to stir the Nuka daily (whether you're pickling vegetables or not) and, once a month, replace the Kombu, Garlic/Ginger/chiles and add a cup of Rice bran to keep it from getting too "runny".

Most Japanese homes don't have basements but will have sub-floor areas to store food-stuffs like Nuka especially in the hot summer months. The Nuka mixture may form a White mold – not to worry! Scoop the mold off, add a cup of Rice bran, mix and let "air" for 8 hours, then replace the top.

Rice Bran

(Nuka-Zuke)

1 large-sized wide mouthed glass jar or medium-sized ceramic pot with a tight-fitting lid (plastic, wood, or metal containers won't work for this pickling method)
2 packages (6 cups) of Rice bran (Nuka) from an Asian food market
4-inch strip of dried Kelp (Kombu)
6 cloves Garlic
6 dried Red Chili Peppers (small)
1 tbsp of Seasalt
1 ¾ to 2 cups of cold, fresh water
1 cup chopped Chinese Cabbage (Hokusai)

For fermenting week

1. Wipe kelp (Kombu) clean with a damp paper towel
2. Peel but do not cut garlic
3. In large bowl, combine bran and salt
4. Add water to mixture cup by cup, mixing by hand until mixture has consistency of a thick pancake batter, not too runny but easy to mix by hand
5. Put 2 cups of the moist bran into pickling jar; dried kelp strip (Kombu)
6. Add 2 more cups mixture; add 2 cloves garlic (or a 3-inch piece of peeled, fresh ginger)
7. Add remaining mixture; add dried red peppers
8. Cover with a heavy plate and cover; let rest 24 hours
9. The initial "curing" part of this fermenting process will take a week for the rice bran medium to ripen and be ready for us
10. On the second day, add 1 cup of chopped Chinese cabbage leaves and stir (by hand or wooden spoon)
11. From the third day on, remove the previous days' Chinese cabbage, discard and add 1 cup fresh chopped Chinese cabbage leaves; stir (by hand or wooden spoon); replace heavy plate and cover
12. After a week to ten days the pickling medium should have a distinct aroma and look like thick, wet sand and will be ready to use; if it appears "runny", add a cup of rice bran and continue daily "curing" process for 2-3 more days.

Pickled Vegetables in Nuka
Nukazuke

- *Carrots* (Ninjin), halved lengthwise and cut into 2-inchlengths
- *Japanese Eggplants* (Nasu), unpeeled, pierced randomly with a fork, and cut into segments about one inch-long
- *Chinese Cabbage* (Hokusai)
- *Japanese Cucumbers* (Kyuri), pierced randomly with a fork and cut into segments about an inch-long
- *Broccoli Florets*
- *Daikon Radish*, cut into rounds about ¼ inch thick
- *Japanese Turnips* (Kabu), greens cut off and cut a deep X into the stem area before placing in the Rice bran. Turnip greens can also be pickled

1. Choose two or three vegetables to pickle.
2. Wash vegetables thoroughly peeling carrots or daikon.
3. Bury cleaned, prepared vegetables in cured Nuka mixture, covering them completely for 24 hours only (any longer and they will be inedible)
4. Gently rinse Nuka-bran from pickles and pat dry with paper towels
5. Place on communal dish; individually take pickles to your own dishes and drizzle with soy sauce if desired

Finished pickles are bright in colour, firm & crunchy

Miso & Rice Bran Pickles
Miso-Zuke

This is another lengthy process that ends up in delicious pickles! Dark or light Miso give different flavours to the pickles so the ingredients can be different
medium-sized wide mouthed glass jars or small-sized ceramic pots with a tight-fitting lid (plastic, wood, or metal containers won't work for this pickling method); one is for Red Miso, the other is for White Miso

Vegetables to Pickle in Miso

- *Carrots*, cut into spears about an inch-long, parboil and pat dry before embedding in Red Miso for at least 3 months (preferably longer)
- *Burdock Root* (gobo), cut into spears about an inch-long, parboil and pat dry before embedding in Red Miso for at least 3 months (preferably longer)
- *Asparagus*, parboil and pat dry before embedding in White Miso overnight
- *Beefsteak Leaves* (shiso), embed in red or White Miso for at least 1 month; use chopped as a filling for Rice balls!
- *Daikon Radish*, cut into rounds about ¼ inch thick (you can also cut them into half moon shapes). embed in Red Miso for at least 3 months
- *Japanese Cucumbers* (kyuri), cut into rounds about ½ inch thick, salt, press, then embed in Red or White Miso for at least 4 months

Garlic Pickled in Miso
(Ninniku Miso-Zuke)

12 cloves of Garlic (Ninniku)
1 cup of Red Miso

1. Remove the outer skin from the garlic; parboil the cloves for about 3 minutes
2. Pat dry and then cut the garlic lengthwise into halves
3. Fill small glass jar (or small lidded storage jar) with one cup of red miso
4. Embed garlic in miso, completely covering garlic (add more miso if necessary); cover container and refrigerate 3 months you
5. Remove garlic from miso (just the pieces you will use for the meal)
6. Wash and pat dry before serving; leave remainder of garlic to continue pickling

After all Garlic has been used, remaining can be used to make Miso soup

Pickled Garlic in Soy Sauce
(Niniku Tsukemono)

20 small heads of Garlic
2 dried Red Chiles
5 - inch square Kelp (Kombu)
1 cup Soy Sauce
1 tbsp Sake
1 cup Ichiban Dashi

1. Soak kelp in Dashi for 30 minutes
2. Peel cloves of garlic
3. Cut peppers in half; remove seeds
4. Cut kombu with kitchen scissors into 1/3 to ¼ wide strips
5. Bring soy sauce and sake to boil; remove from heat
6. Put garlic, chilies, and kelp into a heat-proof glass jar
7. Pour soy sauce & sake mixture on top of garlic; let cool to room temperature
8. Cover and let stand over night

Pickled Daikon Radish
(Takuan)

1 gallon + 1 cup fresh, cold water
1 cup Kosher Salt
1 large Daikon radish
3 cups White cider Vinegar

1. In large saucepan, bring 1-gallon water and salt to boil; remove from heat and let cool to room temperature
2. Peel and slice daikon in half lengthwise, then halve again so that it has been quartered lengthwise
3. Place the daikon in a ceramic or glass crock and cover with the brine
4. *It is important that the brine completely cover Daikon*
5. Let the daikon rest covered in brine for 5 days
6. After 5 days, remove daikon from brine and drain; set aside
7. In a saucepan combine 1 cup water, vinegar, and sugar; bring to boil
8. Remove from heat and cool
9. Place drained daikon in a large glass jar and cover with vinegar mix; double this pickling liquid if needed, again the daikon must be completely covered
10. Cover jar; refrigerate for a minimum of 3 days before serving
11. Slice daikon in 1/8 pieces on diagonal; serve on flat communal plate
12. Soy Sauce may be drizzled on these if preferred

Daikon pickles will keep about 2 months

Salted Eggplant
(Shio Nasuzuke)

5 Japanese Eggplants (Nasu)
1 tsp of Seasalt (Umi Shio)

1. Wash eggplants, remove top stems (discard)
2. Slice into ½ - inch rounds on diagonal
3. Place eggplant into pickle press (or large jar with heavy plate)
4. Add one teaspoon of seasalt, mix well by hand
5. Add second teaspoon of seasalt; mix well by hand
6. Add final tbsp of seasalt and mix well by hand
7. Clamp on top of the pickle press and until it pushes down tightly on top layer of vegetables (if using jar, place heavy plate on eggplant with bowl on top for additional weight)
8. Leave under pressure for at least 10 hours (overnight is best)
9. Remove pickles from press; rinse in colander removing Salt
10. Squeeze out excess water
11. Arrange on serving dish

   Soy Sauce can be drizzled on to taste

Salted Cabbage & Carrots
(Kabaji to Ninjin Asazuke)

1 small head of green Cabbage (Kabaji)
1 medium Carrot (Ninjin)
1 Seedless Cucumber or Japanese Cucumber (Kyuri)
4 tbsps of Seasalt (Umi Shio)

1. Wash cabbage; core and cut leaves into 1 inch pieces
2. Peel carrot; julienne into 1-inch-length matchsticks
3. Wash cucumber; julienne into 1-inch-length matchsticks
4. Place vegetable slices into pickle press (or large jar with heavy plate)
5. Add one teaspoon of seasalt, mix well by hand
6. Add second teaspoon of seasalt; mix well by hand
7. Add final tbsp of seasalt and mix well by hand
8. Clamp on top of the pickle press and until it pushes down tightly on top layer of vegetables (if using jar, place heavy plate on vegetables with bowl on top for additional weight)
9. Leave under pressure for at least 10 hours (overnight is best)
10. Remove pickles from press; rinse in colander removing Salt
11. Squeeze out excess water
12. Arrange on serving dish

    Soy Sauce can be drizzled on to taste

RICE DISHES

RICE

Thankfully, these days it's easy to find electric Rice cookers but it's always good to know how to cook White Rice on the stove. For Japanese cooking, short-grain Japanese Calrose Rice is all that I will use – it simply tastes authentic and delicious. There are different settings for White, brown and sushi Rice – they're a great investment!

Stove-top Cooked White Rice
(Gohan no Takikata)

3 cups White Rice
3 ¼ cups fresh, cold water
Pinch of Seasalt

Washing the Rice

1. Put Rice in a medium sized pot.
2. Fill the pot with enough water, twice the amount of the rice. With clean hands, swish the rice around so that the white powder is washed off the rice.
3. Pour out the water carefully, making sure that the rice remains in the pot (use a wire mesh strainer for the easiest way to strain the rice) and repeat this process three times. Drain on final time.
4. Cooking the rice
5. Pour 3 ¼ cups water over rice and soak for 30 minutes.
6. Cover pot with fitted lid.
7. Cook rice over a high heat until the water reaches a boiling point, then lower to medium heat and cook for 2 minutes. Lower heat to simmer for 15 minutes. Turn off heat and remove pot from burner, let rest for 5 minutes.
8. *If you're using a rice cooker, follow the directions in the manual*

Teriyaki Beef Bowl
(Teriyaki Gyu Donburi)

3 cups Cooked Rice
½ lb. Beef Rib Eye Steak, Sliced "paper thin"
1 medium White Onion (Tamanegi)
½ Carrot, julienned (Ninjin)
6 Broccoli Florets
1 cup Cabbage, roughly julienned
1 cup Soy Sauce (Shoyu)
1 cup brown Sugar
1 Garlic clove, minced
½ tsp fresh Ginger, minced
1 tbsp Mirin
1 tbsp Vegetable Oil, divided
1 tsp Cornstarch
¼ cup water
1 Spring Onion, sliced thinly
1 tsp toasted Sesame Seeds

Teriyaki Sauce

1. In a small pan, mix together soy sauce, sugar; bring to a simmer stirring constantly to dissolve sugar
2. Bring to boil; reduce heat to medium
3. Add minced garlic, ginger and mirin; bring to boil stirring constantly
4. Remove from heat

Preparing Meat

1. Cut sliced beef into 3-inch pieces
2. Slice onion in half and then into in ¼-inch slices
3. In a large skillet, heat one half tbsp of vegetable oil
4. Stir-fry onion, carrots, broccoli, and cabbage until tender crisp; remove from pan with slotted spoon
5. Add remaining half tbsp of vegetable oil to pan
6. Stir-fry beef slices until cooked; remove meat with slotted spoon and set aside
7. Pour teriyaki sauce into pan, stirring quickly
8. Return the cooked Beef and vegetables to the pan and stir gently to coat with the sauce.
9. Place 1 cup hot, cooked rice in each bowl
10. Place cooked vegetables and meat on top of rice
11. Pour on a small amount of thickened teriyaki sauce on each serving
12. Sprinkle with toasted sesame seeds and sliced spring onions

Teriyaki Chicken Bowl
(Teriyaki Toridonburi)

3 cups Cooked Rice
1 lb. Chicken Thighs
1 medium White (Tamanegi)
½ Carrot, julienned (Ninjin)
6 Broccoli florets
1 cup Cabbage, roughly julienned
1 cup Soy Sauce (Shoyu)
1 cup Brown Sugar
1 Garlic Clove, minced
½ tsp fresh Ginger, minced
1 tbsp Mirin
1 tbsp Vegetable Oil, divided
1 tsp Cornstarch
¼ cup water
1 Spring Onions, Sliced thinly
1 tsp toasted Sesame Seeds

Teriyaki Sauce

1. In a small pan, mix together soy sauce, sugar; bring to a simmer stirring constantly to dissolve sugar
2. Bring to boil; reduce heat to medium
3. Add minced garlic, ginger and mirin; bring to boil stirring constantly
4. Remove from heat

Preparing Meat

1. Cut chicken into bite-sized chunks
2. Slice onion in half and then into in ¼-inch slices
3. In a large skillet, heat one half tbsp of Vegetable Oil
4. Stir-fry onion, carrots, broccoli, and cabbage until tender crisp; remove from pan with slotted spoon
5. Add remaining half tbsp of vegetable oil to pan
6. Stir-fry chicken until cooked; remove meat with slotted spoon and set aside
7. Pour teriyaki sauce into pan, stirring quickly
8. Return the cooked chicken and vegetables to the pan and stir gently to coat with the sauce
9. Place 1 cup hot, cooked rice in each bowl
10. Place cooked vegetables and meat on top of rice
11. Pour on a small amount of thickened teriyaki sauce on each serving
12. Sprinkle with toasted sesame seeds and sliced spring onions

Beef Bowl
(Gyu Don)

3 cups Cooked Rice
½ pound thinly Sliced Beef (Gyu Niku)
1 medium Onion (Tamanegi)
1 bunch washed Spinach (Horenso)
4 Eggs

Sauce

3 cups cold, fresh water
1 tsp Dashi no moto
1 tbsp Sugar
1 tbsp Mirin
1 tbsp Soy Sauce (Shoyu)

1. Cut thinly-sliced beef into 3-inch pieces
2. Cut onion in half and then into ¼ inch slices
3. Blanch and drain spinach, cool
4. Squeeze excess water out of spinach, slice into 1 inch pieces
5. Bring water with dashi no moto to a boil
6. Add sugar, mirin and soy sauce; simmer until broth is reduced by half
7. Add beef and onions; boil for 5 minutes
8. Add spinach
9. Beat eggs and pour onto simmering sauce mixture; cover until cooked
10. Place 1 cup cooked rice into each bowl
11. Top with cooked beef and egg mixture
12. *Shirataki Noodles are sometimes used in place of the Spinach*

Chicken and Egg "Family Bowl"
(Oyako-Donburi)

3 cups Cooked Rice
½ lb skinless, boneless Chicken Thighs
1 medium Onion (Tamanegi)
3 Eggs (Tamago)
3 tbsp Seaweed Paper Sliced thinly (toasted Nori, shredded)
3 tbsp thinly Sliced Spring Onion (long Spring onions, Negi)

Sauce

3 cups Ichiban Dashi
1 tbsp Sugar
1 tbsp Mirin
1 tbsp Soy Sauce (Shoyu)

1. Cut chicken into bite sized chunks.
2. Slice onion in half and then into in ¼ inch slices
3. Place sauce ingredients in a shallow pan with chicken and onion
4. Cover and simmer until chicken is done
5. Beat eggs and pour on top of chicken/ sauce mixture; simmer until cooked
6. Put 1 cup of hot, cooked rice into each bowl
7. Divide chicken/ egg mixture equally on top of rice
8. Place 1 tsp seaweed in the middle of each bowl

Deep-Fried Pork Bowl
(Katsu Don)

3 cups Cooked Rice 1 medium
3 Deep Fried Pork Cutlets
1 tbsp Sesame Oil
4 Eggs (Tamago)
3 tbsp Dry Seaweed (toasted Nori, shredded or flaked)
See Deep Fried Pork Culet Tonkatsu recipe page 71

Sauce

3 cups Ichiban Dashi

1 tbsp Sugar (Sato)

1 tbsp Mirin

1 tbsp Soy Sauce (Shoyu)

Preparing the Sauce

1. Cut the onion in half first, then into about ¼ inch thick slices
2. Fry in sesame oil until they become translucent, be careful not to burn them
3. Mix sake and mirin in a small pan and bring to boil; add sugar, soy sauce and Dashi no moto; bring to boil
4. Pour soup on onion and bring to boil and then lower heat to medium
5. Place the cut Tonkatsu in the onion/ soup mixture carefully keeping the shape of the individual pork cutlets; simmer for 2-3 minutes
6. Pour well-beaten eggs over pork and sauce
7. *Make sure the eggs fill the spaces between the pork slices; cover and cook on a medium heat until eggs are fluffy and cooked; do not stir
8. Fill each bowl with 1 cup of hot, cooked rice
9. Top each bowl with a Tonkatsu cutlet and egg mixture
10. Top each bowl with 1 tsp of shredded toasted nori

Raw Fish Bowl
(Kaisen Donburi)

It's easiest to pick up a selection of raw fish (Sashimi) from your favourite Japanese restaurant. Larger Asian food markets will have packaged Sashimi in their refrigerated fish section.

½ Seedless Cucumber or Japanese Cucumber (Kyuri)
6 Shiso Leaves
9 sushi-slices raw tuna (Maguro)
9 sushi-slices raw Salmon (Sake)
9 sushi-slices Mackerel or your favorite Sashimi
3 scallops (Hotate)
3 tsp Japanese Horseradish (Wasabi)
3 tbsp Soy Sauce (Shoyu)
1 sheet of Seaweed paper, shredded (toasted Nori)
Toasted White Sesame Seeds

1. Place one cup of cooked rice into each bowl
2. Using a sharp knife, slice each scallop in half
3. Arrange 3 slices of each raw fish and 2 pieces of scallop on top of the Rice.
4. Sprinkle some toasted shredded Nori over the bowls
5. Sprinkle sesame seeds over each bowl as garnish if desire.
6. Put 1tsp wasabi rolled into a bowl on each to bowl
7. Serve immediately with 1 tsp Soy Sauce in each dipping dish

Tempura Bowl
(Ten-Don)

There are many variations in tempura frying. You can mix two or three vegetables and fry them together for example julienned Carrots and Onion slices. This is called "Kakiage style". Be creative and invent your own style!

3 cups Cooked Rice
2 carrots into thin sticks (i.e. 1 ½ inches long)
1 large Onion, sliced into 1 inch slices
1 large Green Pepper, seeded and cut into ¼ inch rings
1 Sliced Eggplant in ¼ inch rounds
  12 Broccoli florets, soaked in Salted water and dried with paper towel
4 Spring Onions (Spring onions) Sliced lengthwise in half, greens cut off and discarded
1 Zucchini sliced on diagonal in ½ inch chunks
6 washed and de-stemmed Mushrooms, dried with paper towel
12 Green Beans, washed and dried with paper towel
3 stalks Asparagus, cleaned and cut in half
½ Butternut Squash Sliced into ¼ inch thin slices
½ lb. cod cut into 2-inch bite-sized pieces
6 shrimp, peeled, deveined
6 medium scallops, washed and dried with paper towel
1 small squid, sliced into rings or strips OR thawed pre-frozen un-battered calamari

Batter
(Koromo)

Using cold water (about 40F) is a must; this keeps the batter from getting too thick or sticky. Keep the batter in the freezer during frying batches to keep cold. Sticky batter makes for oily tempura

1 Egg, beaten
1 cup very cold (40 F°) water
2 tbsps dry White wine
1 cup Flour

1. Beat the Egg and mix with water
2. Add Flour and whisk quickly
3. Keep batter in refrigerator until using it for frying

Tempura Dipping Sauce
(Tenmen Tsuyu)

1 tbsp Dashi no Moto
1 cup of Water, boiled for two to three minutes
2 tbsps Mirin
1 tbsps Sake
¼ cup Soy Sauce (Shoyu)
Ginger root to taste, freshly grated (optional)

1. Pour water in saucepan and add Dashi no moto
2. Stir occasionally until boiling; lower heat and add the rest of the ingredients
3. Remove from heat
   This can be bought bottled or you can make it (it tastes so much better!)

Tempura Frying Tips

* It's good idea to do trial frying in the beginning. Taste it and decide how long it will have to be fried. Once you get the timing right, the rest is simple.
* If it's difficult to handle the vegetable chunks, you may use a tbsp to drop them in.
* Make sure the batter remains cold while you deep fry by placing the batter bowl on top of a bowl of Rice cubes
* Dip shrimp in the batter by holding the tail, and only fry two or three at a time.
* Dredge fish in Flour before dipping in batter

Deep Frying Tempura

1. Heat the oil to 350°F
2. Dip the vegetables or fish in the batter and place them in the oil
3. Do not fry too many at a time, in order to maintain the temperature.
4. Take the tempura out of the oil just when the batter gets *SLIGHTLY golden* being careful not to over-brown them
5. Vegetables usually take less than two to three minutes.
6. Remove fish when the batter turns very slightly brown.
7. Place one cup hot, Cooked Rice in each bowl
8. Divide tempura fish and vegetables evenly among each bowl
9. Serve with Tenmen tsuyu on the side for dipping.

Mixed Rice Bowl
(Takikomi Gohan)

2 cups Japanese Rice
4 dried Shitake Mushrooms
¼ burdock root (Gobo)
¼ Yam Cake (Konnyaku)
3 inches Carrot (Ninjin)
¼ lb boneless Chicken thigh
1 tbsp Sake
1 tsp Soy Sauce (Shoyu)
1 tbsp Mirin
½ tsp Seasalt

1. Prepare basic white rice recipe; set aside
2. Cut chicken into small pieces; season the chicken with 1 tsp of soy sauce
3. Peel and julienne burdock root thinly; soak in water for 5 minutes; drain
4. Boil Konnyaku once and cut it into small rectangles
5. Peel and julienne carrot
6. Place dried Shiitake Mushrooms to rehydrate; remove stems and slice thinly
7. Place 2 ½ cup of water in a saucepan
8. Add Sake, Mirin, 2 tbsps of soy sauce, and Salt; bring to low boil
9. Add Chicken, Carrot, burdock root, shiitake, and konnyaku
10. Simmer for five minutes, skimming off any foam (Aku) that rises to the surface
11. Remove from heat and cool it
12. Separate the simmered ingredients and the soup, using slotted spoon; set aside
13. Add enough water in the soup return to 2 ½ cups of liquid
14. Put washed Rice in Rice cooker and pour the liquid over the Rice
15. Place simmered ingredients on the top
16. Cook rice as usual
17. Divide equally among small serving bowls

Rice Balls
(Onigiri)

3 cups Cooked Rice
½ tsp Seasalt
6 sheets Seaweed (toasted Nori)

Fillings
Inside: (choose one of for each rice ball)
Pickled Plum (Ume)
Grilled Salted Salmon (small chunks)
Dried Bonito flakes (Katsuoboshi)
Pickled Gourd strips (Kombu Tsukudani)
Flaked canned Tuna (with or without mayonnaise)

Outer Coating

Packaged *or* Homemade Onigiri seasoning (Furikake)

Making Rice Balls

1. Stir ½ tsp seasalt into cooked rice, distributing evenly
2. Cool cooked rice to the point where you can handle it
3. With clean, wet hands (so the rice doesn't stick) place 4 tbsp cooled rice in the palm of one hand
4. Using a finger, make an indentation in the middle of the rice if putting a filling in; place pickled plum or tsp of filling in indentation
5. Cover indentation and filling with 1 tbsp rice
6. Shape rice ball into triangle shape
7. Wrap with seaweed sheet (toasted Nori) and set aside
8. Repeat with rest of cooked rice

OR

1. Make rice balls without inner filling; shape in triangular shape
2. Roll in pre-packed onigiri seasonings or homemade Furikake. Prepackaged Furikake is used for rice balls or simply sprinkled on a bowl of rice. It's high in Salt and MSG, but it's convenient. Check out the different flavours and try them or try to make your own version at home like these:

HOME-MADE FURIKAKE

Salted Sesame Seed Furikake
(Goma Shio)

3 ½ tbsp raw Sesame Seeds (Goma)
1 tsp Seasalt (Umi Shio)
½ cup cold, fresh water

1. Dissolve the Salt in the water, until completely dissolved
2. Spread the Sesame Seeds out in a non-stick skillet
3. Over medium-low heat, stir around until the seeds start to 'pop'.
4. Remove from heat and keep stirring until popping stops
5. Return the pan to the heat; add the Salt water, stirring to distribute evenly
6. Seeds will clump up; keep stirring over a medium-low heat scraping off any Salt that sticks to the pan
7. Stir and scrape until water evaporates
8. *Seeds will be coated with fine Salt crystals and look greyish in colour but no longer clumpy.
9. Remove pan from heat and let the seeds cool in the pan
10. After seeds have cooled down completely and are totally dry, keep stored in an air-tight container.
11. *This will keep fresh for about a month in a cool, dry place

Daikon Leaf, Dried Fish and Dried Shrimp
(Sakura Ebi Furikake)

One bunch of Daikon radish leaves
(about 1 ½ cups after blanching)
1 cup of fine bonito flakes
½ cup Dried Shrimp (Sakura Ebi)
Soy Sauce to taste

1. Wash and pick over the leaves carefully, discarding any discoloured parts. Blanch the leaves in a pot of boiling water, until limp but still bright green; drain leaves and refresh by running cold water over them
2. Squeeze excess water; chop up very finely.
3. Heat up a large non-stick skillet
4. Place chopped leaves, stirring until the leaves are dried out a bit
5. Add bonito flakes and shrimp; sauté
6. Add about 1-2 tbsps of soy sauce; stir until the mixture is somewhat dry
7. Remove from heat and cool
    *Keeps well in the refrigerator for about a week

Salmon Flakes
(Sake Furikake)

½ lb raw Salmon filet with skin
Seasalt
½ cup + 1 tbsp Sake Rice/ cooking wine
1 tbsp Mirin
2 tsp Soy Sauce (Shoyu)

1. Salt both sides of Salmon filet well; leave covered in refrigerator for overnight to Salt fish and draw out moisture as well.
2. Wipe off any excess moisture from Salmon
3. Place Salmon, skin side down, in a dry non-stick skillet
4. Add about ½ cup of sake
5. Cover; let cook over medium heat until the fish is completely steam-cooked and Sake has evaporated
6. Remove salmon from pan; cool and remove skin
7. Flake the fish finely with a fork; remove any fine bones.
8. Wipe out the skillet; return the fish flakes back in the pan
9. Add tbsp of sake, mirin, and soy sauce; stir to evaporate moisture; continue stirring until flakes appear dry and finely flaked, stirring constantly so as not to burn them
10. Cool flakes completely
11. Store in the refrigerator for about 2 weeks in air-tight container

Dried Seaweed and Egg
(Noritama Furikake)

1 ½ cups fine bonito flakes
3 to 4 large sheets of dried Seaweed (toasted Nori)
1 tbsp Sesame Seeds (Goma)
2 shelled Hard boiled Eggs
2 to 4 tbsps Soy Sauce (Shoyu)
1 tbsp Mirin
Pinch of Seasalt

1. Preheat the oven to 300°F / 150°C.
2. Crumple up the bonito flakes into large bowl
3. Crumple up the nori sheets and add to bonito
4. Mix well with the soy sauce and mirin.
5. On a non-stick baking sheet spread the mixture out thinly
6. Put in the oven and bake for 10-15 minutes
7. *Watch carefully; if it starts to smell in the least bit like burned soy sauce, take it out.
8. Remove yolks from hardboiled eggs; push yolks through a fine-meshed sieve onto non- stick skillet
9. *Sieved yolk should resemble fine grains
10. Over a low heat with a pinch of seasalt let the yolks dry out slowly.
11. Gently shake pan frequently to loosen up the yolk grains until dry, about 15-20 minutes being careful not to let them brown; remove from pan to cool
12. Check on the oven frequently to be sure bonito flake-nori is baking but not burning; toss with spatula and return to the oven to ensure even baking; when done, remove from heat and cool
13. Toast Sesame Seeds in a dry pan until seeds begin to pop; remove from heat and cool
14. When the bonito-nori mixture is cooled, crumble it up with your hands as finely as possible or put it in a food processor and pulse-mix until it's fairly fine like the Egg grains (but not a power); place in bowl
15. Mix in the cooled dried out Egg yolk and toasted Sesame Seeds
16. Store in an airtight container in the refrigerator for about a week

Bacon Furikake

½ lb lean, low-fatty Bacon or Proscuitto Ham
1 tbsp Mirin
1 tbsp Raw Cane Sugar (or regular Sugar)
½ tbsp Soy Sauce (Shoyu)
Optional: ¼ tsp Japanese 7 spice (Shichimi)

1. Chop bacon quite finely
2. In skillet, sauté the bacon over a low-medium heat until crispy and rendered of its fat but not burned.
3. Drain the bacon on paper towel
4. Wipe all bacon fat from pan
5. Add other ingredients over medium heat, stirring until the sugar is melted
6. Return the bacon and stir until the liquid has evaporated
7. Remove from heat and cool completely
8. If it is considerably chunky, whirl it in food processor until very finely chopped (but not powdered)
9. Add Japanese 7 spice if using; toss to distribute evenly
10. Store in air-tight container
11. *This will keep in the refrigerator for a week or two

Grilled Rice Balls
(Yaki Onigiri)

3 cups Cooked Rice
3 - 4 Tbsp Soy Sauce (Shoyu)
¼ tsp oil

1. Prepare rice and rice balls for standard rice ball recipe
2. Lightly oil a large nonstick skillet on low heat
3. Place rice balls in the skillet and cook until lightly browned on both sides
4. Brush soy sauce lightly on Rice balls; flip each rice ball over as you brush the Soy Sauce on it; cook about 1 minute
5. Brush Soy Sauce on the other sides and repeat
6. Remove from heat and cool

Green Tea and Pickles on Rice
(Ochazuke)

2 ¼ cups hot, Cooked Rice
1 Salmon filet
½ tsp Seasalt
3 cups Hot Japanese Green Tea

1. Season salmon with salt and leave for 10 minutes
2. Broil or grill 5-6 minutes, until slightly brown
3. Remove the skin and bones, if any, and break into flakes.
4. Put the Rice in each bowl
5. Place flaked Salmon onto each bowl
6. Cover with hot green tea

SIMPLE SUSHI

SIMPLE SUSHI

Stove-Top Sushi Rice
(Sushi Meshi)

3 cups White Rice
3 ¼ cups fresh, cold water
5 inch strip of Kombu (dried Kelp)
1 Tbsp Sake

Sushi Rice Seasoning Mixture

(Prepare before adding to cooked sushi rice)
*Pre-mixed sushi Rice seasoning can be bought at Asian food stores.

4 ½ tbsp Rice Vinegar
1 ½ tsp Seasalt
2 tbsp Sugar

1. Wash the rice as when you are preparing white rice.
2. Put rice in a medium sized pot.
3. Use a damp paper towel to wipe the white powder off the kombu strip
4. Pour 3 ¼ cups water over rice, place the Kombu strip on top of the rice and soak for 30minutes.
5. Remove the kombu strip and add the tbsp of sake
6. Cover pot with fitted lid.
7. Cook rice over a high heat until the water reaches a boiling point, then lower to medium heat and cook for 2 minutes. Lower heat to simmer for 15 minutes. Turn off heat and remove pot from burner, let rest for 5 minutes.
8. Place rice in baking pan or shallow bowl and fan rice to cool it
9. Add seasoning mixture over cooked rice, mixing throughout the rice

*If you're using a rice cooker, follow the directions in the manual and add seasoning to cooked rice

Tips for making Sushi

For me, I like to keep a bowl of cold water to keep the Rice from sticking to my hands in between forming the Sushi, depending on the style I'm making.

Slicing Sushi Rolls

1. Use a non-serrated, sharp cutting knife
2. Hold the roll with bent fingers so as
3. to keep your finger-tips curled away from
4. the blade of the knife
5. Use a sawing motion back and forth, just like sawing a log
6. Wipe your blade clean every three or four cuts to prevent the blade from dragging the Rice and the filling

Dipping Sauce for Sushi

The dipping sauce for sushi is a simple combination of soy sauce with a small bit of Wasabi (a Japanese horseradish) paste that can bought in a tube at your Asian food market. Wasabi is powerfully hot; it's smart to start with a tiny bit of Wasabi mixed into a tbsp of soy sauce in a small, shallow dish. I was told that Wasabi kills the parasites that are in raw fish, so it's a double-duty necessity for eating sushi!

Rolled Sweet Egg
(Tamagoyaki)

This is so much better than it sounds and it's my kids' favourite kind of sushi topping. It's easiest to cook it in the rectangular Japanese skillet, but a small omelet pan can be used.

The Bamboo rolling mat is important for making Tamago; it helps form the square block as the Tamago cools.

4 large Eggs
4 tbsps Ichiban Dashi
2 tbsps Sugar (Sato) 1 teaspoon Mirin
½ teaspoon Soy Sauce (Shoyu) Seasalt

1. Beat eggs thoroughly
2. Add dashi, sugar, Mirin and soy sauce
3. Heat skillet or Tamago pan on medium heat
4. Pour about ¼ of the mixture into a well-oiled Tamago pan
5. Spread a thin layer to cover the bottom of the pan
6. As mixture cooks, bubbles and sets, flip half over and slide it to back of the pan
7. Add more oil to pan and some more of mixture, making sure to get some under the roll
8. As it cooks, roll old roll back to the front of pan, then again to back

9. Repeat until you are out of Egg mixture
10. Remove roll from the pan and place on bamboo rolling mat
11. Pull Bamboo roller around Tamago block to form a rectangle shape and slip a rubber band around it to hold it into place
12. Place on a plate and chill in the refrigerator for 2 hours
13. Remove rubber band, place cold Tamago block on a clean cutting board
14. Slice into 1/8-inch slices; arrange on serving plate with grated Daikon or use as topping for Sushi dishes

Sweet Sushi Shrimp
(Amaebi)

12 medium sized raw Shrimp

1. Shell the shrimp, leaving the tails on 12 toothpicks
2. De-vein them by slicing shallowly along the back and pulling out the dorsal vein
3. Skewer shrimp with toothpicks through the shrimp, straightening them out as you go to the shrimp from curling up when you cook them
4. Bring a small pot of water to a boil and stick the skewered shrimp in for about two minutes to cook
5. Remove from boiling water with a slotted spoon, let cool
6. Slice underside from tail to neck cutting almost to but not through the back and open like Butterflies
7. Place on Nigiri

Tofu Pouches
(Inarizushi)

3 cups cooked & seasoned Sushi Rice
12 sheets Aburaage Tofu pouches (can be bought in the refrigerated section of an Asian food store)

1. Open Inarizushi Tofu pouch bag and (with clean hands) squeeze excess liquid from the pouches.
2. Carefully open the pouches without tearing them.
3. With clean hands, use 2 tbsps of sushi rice and squeeze/ roll into a small oval ball
4. Place Rice ball into Tofu pouch

Cucumber Roll
(Kappa Maki)

3 sheets of toasted nori (dried Seaweed), cut in half
4 cups cooked & seasoned Sushi Rice
Japanese (or English seedless) cucumber, peeled and cut into long sticks (the length of the roll)

1. Put a half-sheet of toasted nori on top of a bamboo mat (Makisu).
2. Spread about a half cup of sushi rice on top of the toasted nori
3. Place cucumber sticks lengthwise on the Rice
4. Roll up the bamboo mat, pressing forward to shape the sushi into a cylinder
5. Press the bamboo mat firmly with hands
6. Unwrap the bamboo mat
7. Cut the sushi roll into bite-size pieces

Tuna Roll
(Maguro Maki)

2 cups sushi Rice
2 sheets of toasted Nori (dried Seaweed), cut in half
4 oz Sashimi-Grade raw Tuna (Maguro)

1. Cut tuna (Maguro) into thin and long sticks
2. Put a toasted nori sheet on top of a bamboo mat (Makisu)
3. Spread the sushi rice on top of the toasted nori sheet
4. Place tuna (Maguro) lengthwise on the rice
5. Roll up the bamboo mat, pressing forward to shape the sushi into a cylinder
6. Press the bamboo mat firmly and remove it from the sushi
7. Cut the rolled sushi into bite-sized pieces

California Roll
(Kali Maki)

2 cups cooked & seasoned Sushi Rice
2 sheets of toasted Nori (dried Seaweed)
1 ripe Avocado
3/4 cup Crab Meat
2 tbsp Mayonnaise
½ tsp Seasalt

1. Peel the avocado and cut if into strips
2. Drain imitation crab and put in a bowl and mix with seasalt and mayonnaise
3. Put a sheet of dried seaweed on top of the mat
4. Spread sushi rice on top of the seaweed and press firmly
5. Sprinkle sesame seeds over the sushi rice
6. Turn the sushi layer over so that the seaweed is on top
7. Place avocado and crab lengthwise on the seaweed
8. Roll the bamboo mat forward, pressing the ingredients inside the cylinder-shaped sushi
9. Press the bamboo mat firmly with hands, and then remove the rolled sushi. Cut the sushi roll into bite-size pieces

Nigiri-Sushi

This is the small, individual style that we all associate sushi with. It's easy to make. I usually buy a take-out assorted sashimi plate from a Japanese restaurant and prepare the sushi rice at home

3 cups cooked & seasoned Sushi Rice
1 Sashimi plate (from your favourite Japanese restaurant) OR Blocks of raw fish (Salmon, tuna (Maguro) etc)
Wasabi

Shaping the "Sushi Fingers"

1. With wet hands, place two tbsps of prepared sushi rice in the palm of one hand
2. Roll the Rice, shaping it into 2 inch log about an inch in diameter these become the base of the sushi.

Preparing the Raw Fish

If you've bought a sashimi plate from a supermarket, the raw fish will already be sliced and prepared for you. If you're cutting raw fish from a block purchased especially for sushi, be sure that your cutting area is clean; keep the fish refrigerated until you're ready to use it.

1. Cut the fish 1/8-inch thickness
2. Place a small dab of Wasabi on the underside of the slice of fish and place it on a Sushi finger
3. Place on a plate in a symmetrical pattern

Sushi Cones
(Temaki Sushi)

3 cups cooked and seasoned Sushi Rice
6 sheets toasted Seaweed (Nori)

Dipping Sauce

3 tbsp Soy Sauce (Shoyu)
1 ½ tsp Wasabi

1. Place 1 tbsp soy sauce in each small dipping dish
2. Add ¼ tsp wasabi and mix (adjust to taste)

Making Sushi cones

1. Take one sheet of toasted nori paper and place it in the palm of your hand
2. *The rough side should be facing you
3. Place 2 tbsp sushi rice on the bottom half of the nori sheet
4. Place a thin line of wasabi on the rice (adjust to taste)
5. Spoon fillings near the center of the rice, laying them diagonally
6. Place the larger items on the bottom and the smaller ones on the top
7. Roll bottom right-hand corner of the nori up and over the rice and fillings diagonally
8. Continue rolling until you form a cone
9. *Makes 6 cones

Dipping Sauce

4 tbsp Soy Sauce (Shoyu)
1 ½ tsp Wasabi

1. Place 1 tbsp soy sauce in each small dipping dish
2. Add ¼ tsp Wasabi and mix (adjust to taste

Dynamite Sauce

¼ tsp of Kewpie Mayonnaise
1 tsp Masago (fish Eggs)
½ tsp Sriracha Hot Sauce

1. Combine ingredients.

*The Kewpie will absorb some of the heat so adjust to taste.
**If you're mixing this with fish, cut the fish into nibble-sized pieces first, about ¼-inch.

Spicy Sauce

¼ tsp of Kewpie Mayonnaise
1 tsp Masago
½ tsp Sriracha Hot Sauce
¼ tsp Sesame Seed oil
¼ tsp Red Chili Pepper flakes
¼ tsp White Sesame Seeds

Fillings

Cucumber

1 seedless or Japanese Cucumber (Kyuri)
½ tsp White Sesame Seeds

1. Slice cucumber into thin lengths about ¼ inch wide, 4 inches long
2. Place cucumber on cooked & seasoned sushi rice; sprinkle with sesame seeds
3. Roll as per directions

Sweet Egg Maki
(Tamago)

1 block prepared Sweet Egg (Tamagoyaki)

1. Slice Tamagoyaki into thin lengths about ¼ inch wide, 4 inches long
2. Place on cooked & seasoned sushi rice
3. Roll as per directions

Pickled Daikon Maki
(Takuan)

1 x 4-inch piece of Takuan (pickled Daikon)

1. Halve Takuan lengthwise
2. Slice each half lengthwise into thin lengths about ½ inch wide, 4 inches long
3. Place on cooked & seasoned sushi rice
4. Roll as per directions

Spicy Tuna

2 blocks Raw Tuna (4 ounces per roll)
1 seedless English Cucumber or Japanese Cucumber (Kyuri)
1 tbsp Spicy Sauce

1. Slice cucumber into thin lengths about ¼ inch wide, 4 inches long
2. Slice tuna into thin lengths about ¼ inch wide, 4 inches long
3. In a small glass bowl, mix tuna with Spicy Sauce
4. Place tuna mix on sushi rice and top with cucumber slices
5. Roll as per directions

Spicy Salmon

Raw Salmon (4 ounces per roll)

1 seedless English cucumber or Japanese cucumber (Kyuri)
1 tbsp Dynamite Sauce

1. Slice cucumber into thin lengths about ¼ inch wide, 4 inches long
2. In a small glass bowl, mix salmon with Dynamite Sauce
3. Place salmon mix on cooked & seasoned sushi rice and top with cucumber slices
4. Roll as per directions

Spicy Scallop

Raw Scallops (4 ounces per roll)
1 seedless or Japanese Cucumber (Kyuri)
1 avocado
1 tbsp Dynamite Sauce

1. Cut scallops into quarters
2. In small glass bowl, mix chopped scallops with Dynamite Sauce
3. Peel avocado and slice into strips ¼ inch wide, 4 inches long
4. Slice cucumber into thin lengths about ¼ inch wide, 4 inches long
5. Place Scallop mix on sushi rice and top with avocado and cucumber slices
6. Roll as per directions

California Roll

1 whole Imitation Crab strip (they come in a package)
1 seedless or Japanese Cucumber (Kyuri)
1 Avocado
1 tbsp Kewpie (or regular) Mayonnaise
1 tsp White Sesame Seeds

1. Cut imitation crab into quarters lengthwise
2. In small glass bowl, mix imitation crab with Kewpie Mayonnaise (or regular mayonnaise)
3. Peel avocado and slice into strips ¼ inch wide, 4 inches long
4. Slice cucumber into thin lengths about ¼ inch wide, 4 inches long
5. Place imitation crab mix on sushi rice; sprinkle white sesame seeds on top
6. Place avocado and cucumber slices on top
7. Roll as per directions

Scattered Sushi Bowl
(Chirashi Sushi)

2 cups of Sushi Rice
3 Eggs
½ cups Toasted Nori (dried Seaweed sheets, shredded into small strips)
½ cups Daikon Radish, shredded
3 Shiso leaves
3 Mackerel Sashimi, sliced
3 Imitation Crab sticks (Kami Kani)
3 medium Shrimp (Ebi)
3 Tuna Sashimi, sliced (Maguro)
15 slices Japanese Cucumber (Kyuru(
3 tbsp pickled Ginger (Gari)
3 tbsp Salmon Roe
3 tbsp Flying Fish Eggs (Tobiko)
3 medium bunches White Baby Radish Sprouts (Kaiware)
3 tsp Wasabi

1. Beat egg and pour into a pre-heated pan with some vegetable oil
2. Move pan around to evenly distribute the egg and make it very thin
3. Once both sides are cooked, remove egg sheet on bamboo mat; cool
4. Julienne cooked egg into thin slices; set aside
5. Fill each bowl with about a cup of rice and flattened in bowl.
6. Add seaweed shreds to cover rice
7. Place julienned egg on top of the seaweed
8. Take about a half a cup of shredded daikon and place it in the back of each bowl in a small mound
9. Place a single shiso leaf and artfully lean it against the daikon mound.
10. Place sliced mackerel on left side of each dish, followed by putting sliced crab sticks in front of it
11. Place a shrimp centred in front of the shiso leaf
12. On right side, place a slice of salmon and then partially cover with a slice of tuna (Maguro) in front
13. Place five pieces of thinly sliced cucumber and arrange fanned out over bottom of each bowl
14. Place a little pickled ginger and Salmon fish eggs on bottom right the bowl
15. Place a spoonful of Tobiko (Flying Fish roe) where Kani-Kami, shrimp and cucumbers meet
16. Place a small bunch of white radish baby sprouts (or Kaiware) on left of Tobiko

SALADS & DRESSINGS

SALADS & DRESSINGS

Green Salad
(Gurinu Salada)

1 ½ cups lettuce
3 small tomatoes
1 seedless English Cucumber or 3 small Japanese Cucumbers (Kyuri)
1 small Carrot (Ninjin)
¼ cup dried Sea Grass (Wakame)
3 hard boiled Eggs
1 tsp Seasalt (Umi Shio)
1 tsp black Sesame Seeds
1 can salmon chunks, drained (optional)

1. Wash lettuce and drain in colander; shred in
2. ½-inch pieces
3. Shell and rinse hardboiled eggs; set aside
4. Boil wakame for 1-2 minutes, drain in colander and rinse with cold water; squeeze out excess water and set aside
5. Wash tomatoes and slice into 6 wedges
6. Wash cucumber, place seasalt on wet cutting board and rub cucumber against salt roughly removing most green skin
7. Remove excess seasalt (Umi Shio) from cucumber; on clean cutting board, slice cucumber in half lengthwise
8. Slice cucumber in to 3-inch-long, 1 inch wide lengths; set aside
9. Peel carrot; shred with mandolin, about ¼ cup
10. Slice each egg in quarter wedges
11. Divide lettuce between individual serving plates
12. Divide boiled Wakame between plates in the center of lettuce
13. Line outer side of plates with tomato wedges, alternating with egg wedges
14. Divide cucumber slices among plates and place in small amounts around wakame
15. Sprinkle salmon chunks over salad
16. Sprinkle black sesame seeds over cucumbers
17. Sprinkle shredded carrot over each plate

Seared Beef Salad
(BIfu Tataki Salada)

3/4 lb. thinly sliced Beef
½ Onion (Tamanegi)
1 Carrot (Ninjin)
3 inch Daikon Radish
4 Shiso Leaves
1 Spring Onion (Negi)
Leaf iceberg lettuce, washed

Citrus-Soy Salad Dressing

1 tbsp Soy Sauce (Shoyu)
2 tbsp Rice Wine Vinegar
2 tbsp fresh Lemon Juice

1. Rub salt and pepper on beef round
2. Grill or pan-sear the beef on all sides until browned but still rare inside
3. Let the beef cool and slice thinly
4. Cut shiso leaves into thin strips; soak in water
5. Peel onion, slice paper-thin
6. Peel carrot, cut in half; julienne into 3-inch long matchsticks
7. Peel Daikon radish; julienne into 3-inch long matchsticks
8. Slice spring onion finely
9. Place lettuce leaf on salad plate for base
10. Place beef slices on a plate and top with vegetables
11. Mix soy sauce, vinegar, and lemon juice dressing; pour over salad

Japanese Potato Salad

3 medium White Potatoes (Imo)
1 small Carrot (Ninjin)
½ Seedless English or 2 small Japanese Cucumber (Kyuri)
1 small Onion (Tamanegi)
1 Egg (Tamago)
Seasalt & Pepper
3/4 to 1 cup of Mayonnaise (Japanese Kewpie brand for the best taste or real mayonnaise)

1. Boil the potatoes in their skins until tender
2. Boil the carrot, unpeeled, in the same pot
3. Boil the egg until hard boiled
4. Slice ends off cucumber
5. Slice the cucumber and the onion paper thin; Sprinkle both with a little salt, and let sit for 10; squeeze firmly to get rid of the juices
6. Drain peel potatoes and carrots while still hot (holding each in a tea towel to peel them)
7. Cut the potatoes into small chunks
8. Slice carrot into small pieces
9. Place potatoes and carrots in medium bowl; toss with a little salt and pepper and leave to cool.
10. Peel the hard-boiled egg and chop up finely
11. When potato and carrot combination has cooled to room temperature, mix in cucumber, onion and egg
12. Mix in the mayonnaise
13. Cover with plastic wrap and cool in the refrigerator for at least one hour

Quick Side Salad

½ Green Cabbage head
1 Carrot

1. Shred cabbage mixed
2. Julienne carrot
3. Toss together

Tofu, Ham, and Cucumber Salad
(Tofu to Hamu to Kyuri Salada)

1 block Firm Tofu (Momendofu
1 cucumber
3 slices Cooked Ham

Dressing
2 tbsp mayonnaise
1 tbsp French dressing
½ tsp Soy Sauce
2 tbsp parsley (finely chopped)
½ tsp salt
Pepper, to taste

1. Cut tofu into ½-inch cubes
2. Cut the ham into ¼ inch squares
3. Slice cucumber into thin rounds; sprinkle with ½ tsp of salt and let sit for about 10 min.
4. When tender, briefly rinse with water and squeeze out any excess moisture.
5. In a bowl, combine the tofu, cucumber, ham and dressing ingredients and the parsley; toss to coat.
6. Chill until served

Japanese Noodles with Vinegar Dressing
(Sunomono)

1 pkg. Shirataki Noodles
1 small Japanese Cucumber, thinly sliced
2 Spring Onions, sliced thinly diagonally
2 oz. Crabmeat
2 tsp. Brown Sugar
3 tbsp. Rice Vinegar
1 tsp. Soy Sauce
1 tsp. Sake
Pinch of salt
Freshly grated Ginger (optional)

1. Combine sugar, vinegar, soy sauce, sake, salt and ginger (if using) in a small bowl; Set aside
2. Parboil noodles, rinse with cold water, and squeeze out excess water
3. Add noodles, cucumber, green onions and crab to a medium sized bowl. Pour sauce over noodles and mix well until thoroughly combined
4. Refrigerate until chilled

Serve in small, individual bowls

Miso Salad Dressing

¾ cup Red Miso (Aka Miso)
3 tbsp Sugar (Sato)
¼ tsp Sesame Oil (Goma Abura)

1. Combine miso and sugar in medium bowl
2. Add mirin, water, soy sauce, sesame oil, and sesame seeds; whisk until well mixed
3. Chill until serving

Ginger Salad Dressing

6 tbsp Rice Vinegar
9 tbsp Vegetable Oil
3 tbsp Sesame Oil
3 tbsp Soy Sauce
1 ½ tsp Sugar
3 tsp Sake
1 tbsp grated Ginger

1. Combine all ingredients in a bowl except the oil
2. Gradually and slowly whisk in oil

Refrigerate until use

Vinegar Dressing 1

3 Tbsp Rice Vinegar
1 ½ Tbsp Sugar
1 tsp Soy Sauce (Shoyu) Seasalt to taste

1. Bring 2 cups water to boil; add konnyaku; cook 3 minutes, drain and chill
2. Bring 2 cups water to boil, add shrimp; cook 3 minutes, drain and chill OR drain canned shrimp and chill
3. Peel carrot; julienne into 2-inch-long matchsticks
4. Julienne cucumber into 2-inch-long matchsticks
5. Soak seaweed in boiling water for 2 minutes; drain and chill
6. Mix ingredients for dressing and chill
7. Combine chilled noodles and shrimp in bowl and toss
8. Divide noodles/shrimp between 3 small, shallow dishes
9. Divide seaweed and vegetables evenly among dishes, placing them in small batches on top of the noodles
10. Pour dressing evenly among bowls

Vinegar Dressing 2

3 tbsp Rice Vinegar (Amasu)
2 ½ tbsp Sugar (Sato)
2 tsp Soy Sauce (Shoyu)
1 tsp Seasalt (Umi Shio)
½ tsp Sesame Oil (Goma Abura)
½ tsp Sesame Seeds (Gomae)
3 cups cold, fresh Water

1. Boil tofu in water for 1 minute; remove from heat, drain, and let cool to room temperature
2. Cut Tofu into 1-inch cubes
3. Combine rice vinegar, sugar, soy sauce, salt, and sesame oil in bowl thoroughly, dissolve sugar completely
4. Add tofu to dressing mixture, toss gently; refrigerate
5. Wash and dry cucumbers; slice ends off cucumber and discard
6. Slice cucumbers lengthwise and then into 2-inch pieces
7. Mix chilled tofu with cucumber; place in serving dish
8. Sprinkle sesame seeds on top
9. Chill until served

SIDE DISHES

SIDE DISHES

Nikujaga
(Beef and Potato Stew)

1 Onion
1 Carrot
2 Potatoes
½ lb thinly sliced Beef
1 pkg Shirataki Noodles
9 Snow Pea Pods (or green beans)
1 tbsp Vegetable Oil

Broth
3 cups Dashi Stock
5 tbsp Mirin
5 tbsp Soy Sauce
3 tbsp Sake
2 tbsp Sugar

1. Blanche snow peas in a small saucepan of boiling water (about 1 minute); Drain and rinse cool down with cold water and set aside.
2. Parboil shirataki noodles in boiling water for 2 minutes; Drain and rinse cool down with cold water and set aside.
3. Heat oil in a medium sized pot over medium heat; cook the beef in the oil until browned.
4. Add potatoes and onions; cook and stir until soft, 5 to 7 minutes
5. Add dashi soup, soy sauce, sake, and sugar; low-boil for 10 minutes
6. Add drained shirataki noodles; stir
7. Reduce heat to low and cook about 15 minutes more
8. Top the mixture with the snow peas to serve.

Salted Soybean Pods
(Edamame)

1 lb. fresh Edamame in pods, or frozen Edamame in pods
½ tsp Seasalt (Umi Shio)
1 tbsp Seasalt (Umi Shio)
1 tbsp Kosher or coarse seasalt
5 cups water

1. Bring water to boil in deep pan
2. Remove stem ends off Edamame pods; wash Edamame and drain
3. Place Edamame in medium bowl
4. Sprinkle ½ tsp seasalt over Edamame; rub Edamame with seasalt
5. Add 1 tbsp of seasalt to boiling water
6. Add Edamame in the boiling water and boil for 3 to 4 minutes
7. Drain with colander
8. Spread boiled edamame on flat serving dish; sprinkle 1 tbsp of Kosher or coarse seasalt; cool edamame
9. Put cooled, salted edamame in a pretty, medium-sized bowl
10. Each guest should have a small plate or dish to place their own Edamame on
11. Eat Edamame by removing inner bean by hand or with your teeth and discard outer skins

Deep-Fried Potato Patties
(Korokke)

1 lb White Potatoes
¼ lb Ground Beef
½ medium White Onion (Tamanegi)
1 Egg (Tamago)
1 tbsp oil
½ tsp Seasalt (Umi Shio)
¼ tsp black Pepper
Peanut or other oil for deep frying Flour
Japanese Panko (breadcrumbs) (Panko)
2-3 green leaf-lettuce leaves

Sauce

Bottled Tonkatsu sauce ("Bulldog" brand)
<u>OR</u>
Ketchup

Filling

1. Peel the potatoes and cut them into medium sized pieces
2. Boil potatoes until soft and mash in large bowl
3. Mince onion finely
4. Heat 1 tbsp oil in skillet; sauté minced onions over low heat until translucent
5. Add ground beef; sauté with onions until beef is cooked; remove from heat
6. When cool, add beef/onion mix to mashed potatoes
7. Add seasalt and black Pepper, mix well

Making Korokke

1. Using a spoon, take 5 tbsps potato mixture and form oval shapes with your hands
2. Coat each piece with flour
3. Dip each flour-coated piece in beaten egg mixture and coat with Panko
4. Heat deep-frying oil to 350°F in deep pan or wok
5. Carefully put panko crumb-coated Korokke in oil, cooking 2-3 at a time
6. Cook until underside is golden brown; turn Korokke over and cook until both sides are golden brown
7. Remove from oil with slotted spoon to draining rack or paper towel to remove excess oil
8. Repeat with remaining Korokke

Presentation

1. Place lettuce leaves on plate and put Korokke on top of lettuce
2. Each person takes their Korokke from the communal plate and adds sauce to their own liking

Bacon-Asparagus Rolls
(Aspara Beikon)

9 stalks fresh Asparagus
3 slices lean Bacon
3 Wooden Skewers
1 tsp Vegetable Oil
3 sprigs Parsley,
3 small Lemon wedges

1. Slice bacon into 2.5-inch-pieces
2. Clean asparagus, cut off thick bottom ends
3. Steam asparagus until tender; immerse in cold water
4. Drain and pat dry with paper towels
5. Cut each asparagus stalk equally in half
6. Wrap two halves of asparagus with bacon
7. Put 3 sets of bacon on one skewer
8. Heat oil in skillet; sauté bacon-covered asparagus until both sides are crispy
9. Remove from pan to paper towel to drain excess oil
10. Place on skewer on individual serving dish
11. Add on spring of parsley and one lemon wedge to each plate for colour and garnish

Broiled Stuffed Japanese Green Peppers
(Niku Piman)

12 Japanese Green Bell Peppers (Piman)
1 small Onion (Tamanegi)
½ lb Ground Pork
¼ cup Japanese Bread Crumbs (Panko)
1 Egg (Tamago)
¼ tsp Seasalt (Umi Shio)
¼ tsp Pepper
2 tsp Soy Sauce (Shoyu)
1 tsp Vegetable Oil
1 tsp Vegetable Oil
6 Bamboo skewers

1. Soak bamboo skewers in water for 30 minutes
2. Peel onion and mince super-fine
3. In skillet, heat vegetable oil on medium and fry onion until translucent; be sure not to brown
4. Wash green peppers, halve, and remove seeds (discard)
5. Remove cooked onions from skillet; set aside to cool
6. In medium bowl, beat egg
7. Add ground pork and cooled minced onion; mix well
8. Add seasalt, pepper and panko; mix well
9. Spoon meat mixture into cleaned green pepper halves
10. Skewer 2 green pepper halves per each bamboo skewer
11. Brush broiling pan with cooking oil
12. Place skewers meat-side down on broiling pan
13. Broil 10 minutes (until meat is cooked, it depends on the size of the green peppers)
14. Turn green peppers over; brush with soy sauce; return to broil 5 minutes
15. Remove from heat, remove skewers and arrange on serving dishes

Pan Fried Ham & Onion Wraps
(Hamu Negimayaki)

12 Spring Onions (Negi)
6 slices Cooked (luncheon style) Ham
1 tbsp Butter
½ tsp Soy Sauce (Shoyu)
12 toothpicks

1. Wash spring onions, pat dry, cut off root-tops (discard)
2. Cut spring onions into half
3. Parboil spring onions quickly, drain, set aside to cool
4. Cut ham slices in half
5. Wrap 1 spring onion top and bottom half with ham slice tightly; secure/ skewer with toothpick
6. Heat butter skillet over medium heat
7. Place rolls in skillet; leave until bottoms are browned; turn over to brown other side
8. Add soy sauce and sauté both sides for 1 minute
9. Remove from skillet to small plate

Deep-Fried Natto
(Natto Karage)

3 packages fermented soybeans (Natto) and included sauce packages (Tare)
1 tsp Soy Sauce
2 blocks silken Tofu (Tofu)
1 Egg (Tamago)
½ cup Potato Starch
2 tbsp Spring Onion (Negi) Oil for deep frying

Ponzu Dipping Sauce

1/3 cup Soy Sauce (Shoyu)
¼ cup Lemon juice
1 tbsp Rice Vinegar (Amasu)
1/3 cup Ichiban Dashi
Combine ingredients, mix thoroughly and chill

Optional
7-Pepper spice (Shichimi)
Japanese mustard (Karashi)

1. Drain tofu; line plate with paper towels, place tofu on top, layer again with paper towels and place another plate on top to remove excess water (30 minutes)
2. Wash spring onions, chop finely
3. Heat oil to 350°F
4. Place well drained tofu in a medium bowl and mash with fork
5. Mix natto & packaged sauce; mix thoroughly
6. Beat eggs; add spring onion and potato starch
7. Fold natto mixture into egg mixture, mix gently
8. Slide into oil by spoonfuls; fry until red-brown, flip carefully to make sure both sides are cooked; fry in batches of 4-6
9. Remove from oil with slotted spoon onto paper towel lined plate
10. Divide Ponzu sauce between 3 dipping bowls; Shichimi (7-pepper mix) or Karashi (Japanese mustard) can be added to ponzu to taste

Sesame Beef & Green Beans

½ lb thinly Sliced Beef
¼ lb Green Beans (Sayaingen)
2 tsp Soy Sauce (Shoyu)
2 tsp Mirin
1 tsp Brown Sugar
1 tsp Sesame Oil (Goma Abura)
2 tsp White Sesame Seeds (Gomae)
*Beef should be Sliced paper thin

1. Place beef in medium bowl
2. Add soy sauce, Mirin, brown sugar and sesame oil; mix thoroughly
3. Let marinate in refrigerator 6 hours
4. Take ends and strings off green beans; wash & pat dry
5. In skillet over high heat 1 tsp sesame oil
6. Add green beans; stir fry 1-2 minutes until crisp and bright green
7. Add sliced beef; stir fry until meat is thoroughly cooked
8. Serve on communal plate

Braised Burdock Root & Carrots
(Kimpira Gobo)

2 Burdock Roots (Gobo)
2 small or 1 medium Carrots (Ninjin)
1 tbsp Sesame Oil (Goma Abura)
1 tsp dry Red Chili Pepper flakes (Ichi-Mi)
1 tbsp Sugar (Sato)
1 tbsp Mirin
1 to 3 tbsp Soy Sauce (Shoyu)

1. Peel burdock root; slice each piece lengthwise; julienne into matchsticks 2 ½ inches long
2. Place burdock root pieces in a bowl with enough water to cover, and let soak for 5 minutes
3. Drain water, and refill the bowl with fresh water; soak 5 minutes more then drain
4. Pat the burdock root dry with paper towels.
5. Peel carrots; julienne into matchsticks 2 ½ inches long
6. Heat sesame oil in wok or large skillet
7. Add the burdock root and carrot pieces, and sauté quickly
8. Add chili pepper flakes and stir fry
9. Add sugar, mirin and soy sauce and about ½ cup of water
10. Lower heat to medium; continue cooking and stirring until the moisture has disappeared from the pan
11. Burdock should be tender crisp when done
*If it's too crunchy, add a bit more water and cook longer
12. Serve in small communal dish

Pan-Fried Dumplings
(Gyoza)

¼ cup chopped Chives (Nira)
1 cup Chinese Cabbage (Hokkusai)
½ lb Ground Pork
1 tsp grated Garlic (Niniku)
1 tsp grated Ginger (Shoga)
1 tsp Sesame Oil (Goma-Abura)
1 tsp Sugar (Sato)
3 tsps Soy Sauce (Shoyu)
20 round Gyoza wrappers (sold in a package)
1 tbsp Vegetable Oil

Dipping Sauce

3 tbsps Soy Sauce (Shoyu)
3 tsp Rice Vinegar (Amasu)
1 ½ tsp Sesame Oil (Goma Abura)

1. Divide ingredients equally among 3 small dipping dishes
2. Wash, pat dry and finely chop chives (to equal ¼ cup); set aside
3. Wash, pat dry and finely chop cabbage (to equal 1 cup); set aside
4. Peel ginger and grate (to equal 1 tsp); set aside
5. Peel garlic and grate (to equal 1 tsp); set aside
6. In large glass bowl, combine chives, cabbage, pork, garlic, ginger, sugar, soy sauce and sesame oil; mix well
7. Fill a small dish with water; keep handy while making Gyoza
8. Place a row of 5 Gyoza wrappers (side by side) on clean, dry cutting board
9. Dip a clean finger in water and run along edge of each wrapper
10. Place a teaspoonful of filling in each gyoza
11. Fold wrapper over filling to make a half-moon shape; pinch edges to seal
12. Repeat with Gyoza wrappers until all filling is used
13. Heat oil on medium in skillet
14. Place Gyoza in skillet; fry on medium heat until bottoms become brown
15. Turn heat to low
16. Add ¼ cup water to pan; cover the pan and steam Gyoza on low heat until water has evaporated
17. Serve Gyoza with dipping sauce on the side

Spring Rolls
(Harumaki)

¼ lb Ground Pork
1 cup Bean Sprouts
12 dried Shiitake Mushrooms
5 oz. thin Bean Sprouts starch Noodles (Harusume) or cellophane Noodles
1 tsp grated Ginger
1 tbsp peanut or Vegetable Oil
1 tbsp Cornstarch
2/3 cup Chicken Soup Stock
1 ½ tbsp Soy Sauce (Shoyu)
1 tsp Sugar
1 tsp Sesame Oil
1 tbsp Sake Rice wine
1 tbsp water and 1 tbsp Cornstarch, mixed
12 Egg roll wrappers
1 tsp Flour and 1 tbsp water, mixed
Peanut or Vegetable Oil of frying

Filling

1. Soak dried shiitake mushrooms in water for 30 min. to rehydrate
2. Cut shiitake into thin strips
3. Boil starch noodles (Harusame) in pan for on minute; drain
4. Cut noodles into 3-inchlengths
5. In a medium glass bowl sprinkle cornstarch over ground pork meat; stir meat
6. Heat 2 tbsp oil in skillet, add ginger and sauté
7. Add ground pork; sauté well
8. Add shiitake strips and bean sprouts; sauté
9. Add chicken soup, sugar, soy sauce, sesame oil, and sake
10. Add starch noodles in the pan and simmer
11. Bring to boil; add water and cornstarch mixture; stir well
12. Remove from heat placing filling into glass bowl; cool

Making the Spring Rolls

1. Place one sheet of wrapper on a clean cutting board so that point are in the 12 o'clock, 6 o'clock, 9 o'clock, 3 o'clock areas like a diamond shape instead of a square.
    *There is a "rough side" and a "smooth side" you want to make sure the "rough side" is up
2. Making imaginary line between the 9 to 3 o'clock points, place 3 tbsp filling below the imaginary line
3. Fold the bottom point over mixture to the imaginary middle point
4. Fold the 3 o'clock point to middle
5. Fold the 9 o'clock point to middle; Spring Roll should look like an open envelope
6. Dip your finger or a cooking brush in water and run it along the open edge of wrapper
7. Carefully roll Spring Roll up; seal
8. Repeat for remaining sheet

Chicken and Cheese Spring Rolls
(Tori Bakonu-Cheezu Harumaki)

12 sheets square Spring Roll wrappers
¼ lb shredded Mozzarella Cheese
¼ lb thinly Sliced Bacon
1 lb boneless, skinless Chicken Filets
3 Green Lettuce Leaves
2 cups Peanut (or other) oil for deep frying

To seal wrapper

1 tbsp water

Dipping Sauce

1 tsp Japanese Mustard (Karashi) (OR packets from Natto)
2 tbs Spicy Sesame Oil
3 tbsp Soy Sauce (Shoyu) (OR the sauce packets from the Natto)

Filling

1. Cut bacon into 3-inchstrips, 1 strip for each Spring Roll
2. Pound filets between parchment paper
3. Cut filets in 3-inch strips, enough for each Spring Roll

Making the Spring Rolls

1. Place one sheet of wrapper on a clean cutting board so that point are in the 12 o'clock, 6 o'clock, 9 o'clock, 3 o'clock areas like a diamond shape instead of a square
2. *There is a "rough side" and a "smooth side" Be sure the "rough side" is face- up*
3. Making an imaginary line between the 9 to 3 o'clock points, place 3 tbsp of the Natto & Rice mixture below the imaginary line
4. Place one slice of chicken, one slice of bacon and 1 tsp grated cheddar below imaginary line
5. Fold the bottom point over the filling to imaginary middle point
6. Fold the 3 o'clock point to middle
7. Fold the 9 o'clock point to the middle; Spring Roll should look like an open envelope
8. Dip your finger or a cooking brush in water and run it along the open edge of wrapper
9. Carefully roll Spring Roll up and seal it
10. Repeat for remaining sheets

Deep Frying the Spring Rolls

1. Place oil in a large saucepan or wok
2. Heat oil over medium heat to 350°
3. Gently place 3 Spring Rolls in the hot oil, turning over when the bottoms are golden brown; fry until both sides are golden brown
4. Remove from oil with a slotted spoon to paper towels to remove excess oil
5. Repeat with remaining Spring Rolls
6. Divide Spring Rolls evenly on flat dishes on a bed of green leaf lettuce
7. Place Soy Sauce or tare and 1/8 tsp Sesame Oil in individual dipping dishes
8. Place 1/8 tsp of Karashi mustard in a Corner of the dish

Fried Potatoes and Bacon
(Baekon-Imo Yaki)

1 lb Potatoes (Jagga Imo)
¼ lb Bacon (Baekon)
1 small Carrot (Ninjin)
1 Green Pepper (Piman)
1 Onion (Tama Negi)
½ cup canned Corn
1 tbsp Butter
Salt & Pepper to taste

1. Boil Potatoes in skin until tender; remove from heat, cool, and remove skins
2. Slice Potatoes in ¼ inch slices
3. Cut bacon into 1-inch slices
4. Cut green pepper in half, seed, and slice thinly
5. Peel carrot; cut in half horizontally; slice thinly on diagonal
6. Peel and cut onion in half; slice in 14-inch slices
7. Heat skillet or wok on medium heat; add bacon
8. Fry bacon until tender but not crisp
9. Add potatoes, carrots, onions, green pepper; stir fry until vegetables are crisp
10. Add corn, sauté one more minute
11. Remove from heat; place mixture on communal dish; sprinkle with Salt and Pepper to taste

Deep Fried Beef with Cheese
(Bifu-Chizu Age)

½ lb thinly Sliced Beef strips
5 tbsp grated Cheddar Cheese
5 tsp Seaweed flakes (flaked toasted Nori)
Oil for deep frying
3 Parsley sprigs
3 Lemon wedges for garnish

Batter

1 cup All Purpose Flour
¼ cup Cold water
1 Egg, beaten

1. Heat oil in deep pan or wok to 350°F
2. Place one strip thinly sliced beef on cutting board
3. Sprinkle ¼ tsp nori flakes on sliced beef
4. Place 1 tsp cheddar cheese at bottom of slice and roll up
5. Mix flour, water and Egg together
6. Dip rolled beef in batter
7. Deep fry in batches until golden brown
8. Divide evenly among 3 individual dishes
9. Place 1 sprig of parsley and 1 lemon wedge on each plate

Green Beans with Miso & Sesame Seeds

½ lb Green Beans (Sayaingen), washed
1 tbsp toasted Sesame Seeds (Gomae)
1 tsp Sugar
1 tsp Miso paste
1 tbsp Soy Sauce (Shoyu)
1 tsp toasted Sesame Seeds for garnish

1. Trim ends from green beans
2. Boil the green beans for 2 mins maximum, drain, place in ice water for 2-3 mins; drain
3. Grind sesame seeds into a coarse paste with a pestle and mortar
4. Add remaining ingredients; continue grinding until smooth
5. Coat with the dressing, garnish with sesame seeds
6. Serve on communal dish

Boiled Japanese Squash (Kabocha Nimono)

1 small Kabocha squash
3 cups Ichiban Dashi
4 tbsp Mirin
2 tbsp Soy Sauce (Shoyu)
1 tbsp Sugar (Sato)
Seasalt -- to taste

1. Wash kabocha squash well, half, remove seeds (discard)
2. Slice kabocha squash into 1-inch strips
3. In saucepan on high heat, bring dashi, mirin, soy sauce, sugar, and salt to a boil
4. Add Kabocha slices, reduce heat to low and cover
5. Simmer until the squash is tender but not mushy
6. Arrange in individual bowls with liquid spooned over

Baked Eggplant with Miso

3/4 cup Red Miso (Aka Miso)
1 Egg yolk (Tamago)
2 tbsp Sake
1 tbsp Mirin
1 tbsp Sugar (or honey)
Japanese Eggplants (Nasu)
Vegetable Oil for brushing

1. Pre-heat oven to 325ºF
2. Combine ingredients for miso mixture into saucepan
3. Over low heat, cooking for 10 minutes, stirring constantly or until mixture thickens and glossy; remove from heat
4. Cut into slices 1½-inch thick; make crosses in flesh with knife
5. Brush oil over eggplant and bake in oven for 10 – 15 mins
6. Cover each piece with 1 tsp miso paste and bake 8 – 12 mins
7. *Be careful not to let the Miso paste burn
8. Serve hot on individual serving dishes

Japanese Pancakes
(Okonomiyaki)

1 cup All Purpose Flour
1 cup Ichiban Dashi
1 large-size Egg (Tamago)
10 leaves Green Cabbage, shredded (Kabbaji)
1 small Onion, Sliced (Tama Negi)
¼ cup Mozzarella Cheese, shredded

Choose from
Thinly-Sliced Beef or pork
Chopped (raw) bacon
Sliced (raw) Shrimp
Calmari/ Octopus rings

Toppings

Mayonnaise
Shredded Seaweed (Aonori)
Dried bonito flakes (Katsuoboshi)
Pickled Ginger (Beni Shoga)

Okonomiyaki Sauce

2 tbsp Tomato Sauce
2 tbsp Ketchup
1/3 cup Worcestershire sauce
3 tbsp Soy Sauce (Shoyu)
1 tsp Sugar (Sato)
7 tbsp Ichiban Dashi
2 tbsp Cornstarch dissolved in 2 tbsp water

1. Bring tomato puree, ketchup, Worcestershire sauce, soy sauce, sugar and dashi to boil in saucepan over high heat
2. Add cornstarch mixture, a little at a time, and cook until thickened to the texture of ketchup cool before serving
3. Mix the flour, egg, and dashi; mix until smooth
4. Stir in the other ingredients except the meat or seafood, mixing well.
5. Heat up an oiled skillet or griddle
6. Cook the meat or seafood in the pan first (about 3-4 slices/ pieces for each separate okonomiyaki)
7. After the meat/seafood is well cooked pour some of batter on top; cook until batter is cooked and then flip over

As each okonomiyaki "pancake" is nearly done, top with cheese and cover until melted

8. Serve with sauce, mayonnaise, aonori (flaked Nori), katsuoboshi (fish flakes) and beni shoga (pink pickled Ginger) on

MEAT DISHES

MEAT DISHES

Deep-Fried Pork Cutlets (Ton-katsu)

1 boneless pork loin chops
2~3 tbsp Flour
1 Egg (Tamago)
Black Pepper to taste
1 ½ cups Japanese Panko (breadcrumbs) (Panko)
Oil for deep frying

Deep Frying Cutlets

9. Make shallow cuts every 3-4 cm crisscrossing the pork loin chops to prevent from curling while frying)
10. Sprinkle with black pepper
11. Beat egg
12. Put Flour, eggs, and Panko (breadcrumbs) in separate dishes for coating the chops
13. Cover with flour, then egg and then Panko (breadcrumbs)
14. Deep-fry at 350°F until Panko (breadcrumbs) are deep golden brown, turn over and cook until that side is also deep golden brown
15. Remove from oil with slotted spoon
16. Slice each piece into 1 ½ inch strips for easy eating

*Serve with shredded cabbage and rice.

Deep-Fried Chicken Cutlets (Chikin-katsu)

3 chicken breast fillets or 6 boneless/ skinless thighs
Salt and pepper
5 tbsp flour
2 eggs, beaten
1.5 cups panko Panko (breadcrumbs))
Oil to deep fry

1. Cut filet horizontally to butterfly
2. Tenderize between two sheets of plastic wrap with meat mallet or dull edge of knife
3. Season with salt and pepper.
4. Place flour, egg and Panko (breadcrumbs) in separate shallow plates and and line them up in this order..
5. Coat each fillet with flour (shake off excess flour); dip both sides in beaten egg; coat liberally with Panko and coat all over. Allow excess egg to drip, then transfer to the Panko (breadcrumbs) liberally.
6. Deep-fry at 350°F until Panko (breadcrumbs) are deep golden brown, turn over and cook until that side is also deep golden brown
7. Remove from oil with slotted spoon
8. Slice each piece into 1 ½ inch strips for easy eating

*Serve with Quick Side Salad and rice.

Pork Spareribs and Radish
(Buta Bara Niku to Daikon no Nikomi)

2½ lbs Pork Rib Meat, deboned
4lbs Daikon Radish
2 cups Sake or White cooking wine
2 tbsp Ginger juice
6-8 cups cold, fresh water
1 cup Soy Sauce (Shoyu)

1. Cut pork meat into 4-unch pieces
2. Fill large pot with water and bring to boil
3. Boil pork meat 2-3 minutes until foam appears on cooking water
4. Drain, rinse with clean water; set aside
5. Wash & peel daikon radish and cut into 2-inchthick rounds
6. Fill large pot with cold water and daikon; bring to boil
7. Remove from heat, drain, and rinse with cold water; set aside
8. In large saucepan combine sake, pork and 1 tbsp Ginger juice stir
9. Add 6-8 cups water – enough to cover pork
10. Bring to boil, reduce heat, cover; simmer 45 minutes
11. Add ½ cup soy sauce, simmer 1 hour
12. Add remaining 12 cup soy sauce and simmer until liquid is reduced by 1 cup
13. Add 1 tbsp ginger juice; stir; serve
14. Serve in communal serving bowl

Grilled Chicken on Skewers
(Yakitori)

½ lb boneless, skinless Chicken Thighs (Tori no momo)
3 Spring Onions (Negi)
9 Bamboo skewers (Take Gushi)

Yakitori Sauce

5 tbsp Soy Sauce (Shoyu)
5 tbsp Mirin
3 tbsp Sugar

1. Soak bamboo skewers in salted water to prevent them from burning on grill
2. Preheat oven to 400°F
3. Place ingredients for Yakitori sauce into a saucepan; simmer until reduced by half
4. Cut chicken into 1.5-inch bite-sized chunks
5. Cut spring onions into 1.5-inch pieces
6. Thread chicken and spring onions onto skewers; alternate chicken chunks & onion pieces
7. Place skewers in a single layer on a greased broiling pan or baking sheet
8. Cook for 5 minutes; brush with Yakitori sauce and return to oven until meat is cooked
9. Place 3 skewers Yakitori on each individual dish
10. Pour remaining sauce over Yakitori

Deep Fried Pork Skewers
(Buta Kushi Katsu)

3 ½ inch thick Pork Loin cutlets
6 Spring Onions (Negi)
1 cup Flour
1 cup Panko Bread Crumbs (Panko)
1 Egg (Tamago)
¼ tsp Seasalt
¼ tsp Pepper
6 Bamboo skewers
Oil for deep frying

1. Place Bamboo skewers in water for 30 minutes
2. Heat oil to 360°F
3. Cut each pork cutlet into 4 pieces
4. Season pork with seasalt & pepper; set aside
5. Wash spring onions; slice off root tip and greens below white part (discard)
6. Cut each spring onion into half; set aside
7. Weave bamboo skewers through pork strips; alternate green Onion (2 halves per skewer)
8. Lightly beat egg; set egg, flour and panko in separate dishes
9. Dip each skewer into flour, then the egg and coat with the panko bread crumbs
10. Press the Panko (breadcrumbs) lightly into the meat
11. Lay the skewers in a single layer
12. Place several skewers into the oil; deep fry until golden brown on all sides
13. Remove from oil to draining rack or plate lined with paper towels
14. Serve with Bulldog Sauce (Tonkatsu) and/or mayonnaise
15. Serve hot, 2 skewers per serving dish

Chicken Balls
(Tori no Tsukune)

½ lb Ground Chicken (Tori Hikiniku)
1 small Onion (Tama Negi)
3 tbsp Sake or White cooking wine
½ tsp Seasalt (Umi Shio)
9 Bamboo skewers (Take Gushi)
Vegetable Oil for deep frying

Sauce

½ cup fresh, cold water
1 tbsp Sake
2 tbsp Sugar
2 tbsp Soy Sauce (Shoyu)
1 tsp Potato starch (Katakuiko)

1. In saucepan, mix all sauce ingredients including potato starch, mixing thoroughly
2. Bring to boil
3. Lower heat and simmer until sauce thickens

Frying Chicken Balls

1. Heat oil to 350°F
2. Peel and mince onion
3. Mix ground chicken, minced onion, salt and sake; mix well
4. Form ½ inch diameter balls (9 or 12 balls)
5. Coat with potato starch
6. Deep fry chicken balls until golden brown
7. Remove from oil with slotted spoon; place on paper towels to remove excess oil
8. Thread 3-4 balls per skewer, placing 3 skewers per individual plate
9. Pour hot sauce over Chicken Balls

Chicken Wings
(Tebasaki)

15 Chicken Wings
1 tsp grated Ginger juice
1 tbsp Sake
Seasalt (Umi Shio)
Potato or Potato Starch

Sauce
2 tbsp Soy Sauce (Shoyu)
1 tbsp Sake
3 tbsp Mirin
2 Tbsp White Sesame Seeds

1. Make a cut along the bone of each chicken wings
2. Put grated ginger, sake, and chicken wings in a plastic bag for 30 minutes
3. Place chicken wings on paper towels and season with salt and pepper on both sides
4. Lightly coat chicken wings with potato or potato starch
5. Heat oil in a deep skillet to about 350°F; fry 4 or 5 chicken wings at a time until golden brown, (about 8 to 10 minutes)
6. Combine ingredients for sauce in a bowl in saucepan and bring to boil
7. Pour on fried Chicken wings in skillet; coat with sauce well
8. Place on communal plate and sprinkle with White Sesame Seeds

Fried Chicken and Fries Basket
(Chikin Karaage Basuketo)

1 lb boneless, skinless Chicken (Tori no Momo)
3 tbs Potato starch (Katakuriko)
Oil for deep frying
3 large White Potatoes
Oil for deep frying

Marinade

2 tbsp Sake
2 tbsp Soy Sauce (Shoyu)
2-inch piece of fresh Ginger (Shoga)

1. Cut chicken into 2-inch chunks
2. Peel ginger and grate; squeeze grated ginger saving juice for marinade
3. Combine ginger juice, soy sauce and sake
4. Marinate chicken in marinade for 1 hour, turning occasionally
5. Heat deep frying oil to 350°F
6. Sprinkle potato starch over chicken, mixing thoroughly
7. Deep fry chicken 3-4 pieces at a time until golden brown

Making Fries

1. Heat deep frying oil to 350°F
2. Wash and peel potatoes
3. Slice into 2-inch-long, ¼ inch wide strips
4. Deep fry in small batches until golden brown
5. Use metal slotted spoon to remove from oil and drain on paper towels
6. Salt while hot

*Serve in individual dishes with freshly made Potato fries

Ground Beef & Vegetables with Cheese
(Bifu-Chizu Kapu)

½ lb Ground Beef
½ cup fresh or frozen Peas & Carrots
¼ cup minced Onion (Tama Negi)
1/3 cup Panko (breadcrumbs) (Panko)
6 tbsp shredded Mozzarella
1 Egg, beaten (Tamago)
1 tsp Ketchup
3 Lettuce leaves
6 Cherry Tomatoes

1. Preheat oven to 350°F
2. Cook peas & carrots until tender; drain
3. Mix 3 tbsp shredded cheese with peas & carrots
4. In medium bowl, mix ground beef, onions, egg, ketchup, and Panko (breadcrumbs); mix well
5. Divide ground Beef mixture among 6-cup muffin tin
6. Pat ground Beef into cups and up sides making a well
7. Fill each ground beef with peas & carrots/ cheese mixture
8. Top each cup with remaining cheese
9. Bake 25-30 minutes until beef is cooked
10. Place 1 lettuce leaf on each individual dish
11. Place 2 ground beef cups on each lettuce leaf
12. Place 2 cherry tomatoes on the side of each plate

Japanese Hamburger Patties
(Wafu Hamubagu)

3 cups Cooked Rice
1 lb Ground Beef
1 Onion (Tama Negi)
1 Egg, beaten (Tamago)
¼ cup Milk
1 cup Panko Panko (breadcrumbs) (Panko)
Seasalt (Umi Shio) & Pepper to season
Vegetable Oil for flying

Sauce

3 Tbsp Ketchup
3 Tbsp Worcestershire Sauce

1. Peel onion and chop finely
2. Heat vegetable oil in a skillet; sauté onion well and set aside
3. Put egg and milk in a bowl and mix well
4. Add panko Panko (breadcrumbs), mix lightly, set aside
5. Put beef in medium bowl; add to cooked onion and breadcrumb mixture
6. Season beef mixture with salt and pepper
7. Mix meat with hands well
8. Make 3 meat balls and toss each ball from one hand to the other hand to remove excess air
9. Make 3 hamburger patties; indent centre of each with finger
10. Heat oil in a skillet and fry hamburgers over medium heat until light brown; turn over, cook until light brown
11. Add ¼ cup of hot water to skillet; over with a lid and steam hamburgers 3-5 minutes Remove and cook until water has evaporated; remove hamburgers and set aside
12. Add ketchup and Worcestershire sauce to skillet

13. Stir quickly over low heat
14. Pour over plated hamburgers
15. Place 1 cup cooked rice on each plate
16. Place one hamburger on each plate
17. Pour sauce over hamburgers
18. Serve hot with green salad on the side

Deep Fried Pork Balls
(Buta no Dango Age)

¼ cup dried Shiitake Mushrooms
1 bunch Spring Onions (Negi)
1 lb Ground Pork
2/3 tsp Seasalt (Umi Shio)
1 tsp Sugar (Sato)
1 Egg (Tamago)
1 tbsp Sake or White cooking wine
Oil for deep frying

Marinating Sauce

4 tbsp Soy Sauce (Shoyu)
3 tbsp Vinegar
1 tbsp Sugar
1 dried Chili Pepper
¼ cup dried Bonito flakes (Katsuoboshi)
6-inch strip dried Kelp (Kombu)

1. In medium saucepan, mix soy sauce, vinegar, sugar, peppers, dried bonito flakes and kelp; bring to boil; remove from heat
2. Heat deep frying oil to 350°F
3. Rehydrate shiitake mushrooms in small bowl of cool water (about 20 minutes)
4. Squeeze excess water out, remove and discard stems; mince caps finely and set aside
5. Mince spring onions, set aside
6. In large bowl, mix pork, minces mushrooms, mince onions, soy sauce, salt, sugar, egg and sake; mix well
7. Form into 1-inchdiameter balls; deep fry; remove with slotted spoon and place on paper towel to remove excess oil
8. Place deep fried pork balls in marinating sauce for 6 hours; remove with slotted spoon to serving dish

Pork Cutlets and Curry
(Katsu Kare)

3 pieces of deep-fried Pork (Tonkatsu)
3 cups Cooked Rice
5 medium-sized Potatoes (Jagga Imo)
2 large Carrots (Ninjin)
1 Onion (Tamanegi)
 Vegetable Oil
Japanese Curry Roux (Kare Roux)
*Buy this in Japanese supermarkets, boxed. There are different brands ranging from mild, medium, medium-hot and hot. They have a deep, creamy curry flavour. The roux is in a block form with easy-to-break small blocks so you can add to make your favourite curry consistency; cooked curry sauce should be a little thicker than soup consistency.

Prepare Tonkatsu recipe
See Deep Fried Pork Culet Tonkatsu recipe page 71

This curry recipe can be used with chicken, pork, or beef cubes but we already have the Tonkatsu for this particular recipe. If you were making curry with meat in it, just cube your choice of meat into pieces the same size as the vegetables

Curry Roux Recipe

1 tsp turmeric
1 tsp cardamom
1 tsp cumin
1 tsp cinnamon
1 tsp cloves
1 tsp garlic powder
1 tsp nutmeg
1 tsp garam masala
1 tsp black pepper
1 tsp ginger powder
1 tsp onion powder
1 tsp chilli powder
1 tsp curry powder
3 tbsp butter
3 tbsp plain (all purpose) flour
3 tbsp honey

1. Roast all selected spices in a non-stick frying pan over low heat for about 5 minutes till fragrant; set aside
2. Melt butter in a frying pan over low heat and add honey
3. Add flour into the frying pan and stir to combine butter and flour
4. Keep stirring for about 15 minutes. The mixture is lumpy at the beginning but will become smooth
5. Add roasted spices into the frying pan; when well combined, remove from heat off
6. Line container(s) with plastic wrap and place the roux into the containers
7. Cover and wrap curry roux with the plastic wrap; make scores so that they easily break into pieces when needed
8. Place in the fridge overnight and allow to set
9. Peel and chop onion in 2-inch slices
10. Peel and chop carrots into 2-inch chunks
11. Peel and chop potatoes into rough chunks (not too small, otherwise they will disintegrate in the cooking process).
12. Heat some vegetable oil in a large saucepan, then fry onion, carrots and potatoes until lightly browned
13. Add water to cover meat and vegetables by half an inch (you can always add more later) and bring to a boil
14. Turn heat down to low and simmer for about 10 to 15 minutes with the lid almost covering the saucepan

Stir occasionally to make sure sticks to the bottom of the pan; add water if necessary, a little at a time. Add 4 small blocks of curry roux

15. Continue to cook over low heat for another 10 minutes, stirring occasionally, until sauce thickens; if it's overly thin for your liking, add another small block of curry roux
16. Place 1 cup on each plate, to the side in an oval shape
17. Place one piece of cooked Tonkatsu in the middle of the place leaning on the Rice
18. Place a ladle of cooked curry sauce on pork with a nice presentation of the vegetable

1.

HOT POTS

HOTPOTS

Hot pots are communal dishes cooked and served at the table. In North America we would use a deep electric frypan; in Japan a small portable camp-stove using canned propane is used. Serve with hot Cooked Rice and pickles

Sukiyaki

1 pound thinly Sliced Beef

*If you can't get thinly-sliced beef from an Asian supermarket ask your butcher to slice sirloin Beef "paper thin" – thinner than bacon

1 package Yam Noodles (Shirataki)
7-8 Shiitake Mushrooms
1 block Enoki Mushrooms
1 Leek (Naga Negi)
½ Chinese Cabbage (Hakusai)
1 block grilled Tofu (Yakidofu) or silken Tofu

Sukiyaki Broth

1/3 cup Soy Sauce (Shoyu)
3 tbsps Sake
5 tbsps Sugar (Sato)
3/4 cup water
1/8 cup Beef Lard or 2 tbsp Vegetable Oil

For Dipping

3 Raw Eggs

1. Drain yam noodles
2. Cut Leek 2 inches below white-end; wash thoroughly; slice in 1/8-inch slices on diagonal
3. Drain Tofu if necessary and cut into 2-inch cubes
4. Cut connective fibery-bottoms of enoki mushrooms, wash, and separate into small clusters
5. Remove stems from shiitake
6. mushrooms; make cross incision on tops
7. Cut thick bottom off Chinese cabbage, wash leaves and chop roughly into 3-inch pieces
8. Mix soy sauce, sake, sugar, and water for Sukiyaki sauce
9. Set electric pan or a skillet in middle of table.
10. Heat lard or vegetable oil in skillet
11. Lightly fry 2 or 3 beef slices; pour Sukiyaki sauce in the pan
12. When the sauce starts to boil, add other ingredients in small amounts
13. Simmer until all ingredients are softened
14. Remove to each person's dish
15. Crack one egg into each person's small egg dish and beat
16. Dip the cooked sukiyaki into the raw, beaten eggs
17. As the liquid boils away, add more sukiyaki sauce
18. On large platter, place drained yam noodles in middle; place other chopped vegetables around yam noodles keeping sliced raw beef on separate plate
19. Have cooked rice available in a separate rice bowl for each person to accompany the Sukiyaki

Beef and Vegetable Hotpot
(Shabu-Shabu)

3 -- inches Dried Kelp (Kombu)
1 lb. Chinese Cabbage (Hakusai)
¼ lb Leeks (Naga Negi)
1 block cotton Tofu, cut into bite-size pieces
1 block Enoki Mushrooms
¼ lb Carrot
1 ½ lb Sirloin Beef, very thinly Sliced (Usugiri Niku)

1. Fill a deep electric skillet or a medium skillet two-thirds full with water
2. Peel carrot; cut into ¼-inch slices on diagonal
3. Soak kombu in the water for 30 minutes
4. Wash hokusai, chop into 2-inch pieces
5. Wash leeks to get sand out, slice diagonally ¼ - inch thickness
6. Wash Enoki mushrooms; cut off fibery-bottom; separate into small bunches
7. Arrange ingredients on a large platter
8. Set the cooking pan in middle of table
9. Heat the water and remove Kombu just before water comes to a boil

To eat

Put a slice of Beef or a vegetable in the boiling soup and swish it gently for a few seconds
Remove from pan and dip in the sauce
Serve with bowls of hot cooked rice
*Skim off any foam (Aku) that rise to the surface as you repeat cooking

Mixed Stew
(Oden)

1 White Radish (Daikon)
1 Yam Cake (Konnyaku)
6 Hard Boiled Eggs (Tamago)
3 Fish Paste Rolls (Chikuwa)
3 deep fried Tofu cakes (Atsuage)
2 Fried Fish Paste Cake with Burdock Root (Gobouten)
2 uncolored Fried Fish Paste Cake usually with Cloud Ear Mushrooms (Shiroten)
9 Fishcake Balls (Age Boru)
2 Fish Paste Cake containing grated Mountain Yam (Hanpen)

*All ingredients can be bought at an Asian supermarket in the frozen food section

Broth

10 cups Water (Mizu)
3 tbsps Sugar (Sato)
3 tbsps Mirin (Sweetened Rice Wine)
3/4 cup light Soy Sauce
1 strip dried Kelp (Kombu)
¼ cup dried Bonito flakes (Katsuoboshi)

Optional

Japanese mustard paste (Karashi) Seven-spice mix (Shichimi)

1. Remove shells from hard-boiled eggs and set aside
2. Peel daikon radish; slice into 1-inch thick rounds
3. Boil daikon in water before simmering it with the other ingredients.
4. Cut konnyaku into triangles; score Konnyaku and boil
5. Parboil Atsuage, Gobouten and Shiroten to remove excess oil. Combine ingredients for broth in large saucepan; heat to boil
6. Strain broth through a cheesecloth lined strainer; discard debris
7. Place all the ingredients except for the Hanpen into the pan and add the strained broth
8. Heat it over high heat to a boil; reduce heat and simmer for two hours ,covered
9. Add Hanpen; cover and simmer until Hanpen has double in sized
10. Serve in communal pot adding Japanese mustard/ seven spice mix individually
11. Serve with cooked rice on the side

Tofu Hotpot
(Yu-Dofu)

4 blocks firm Tofu
4-inch length dried Kelp (Kombu)
8 cups cold, fresh water

Dipping Sauce

3 cups Ichiban Dashi
cup Soy Sauce (Shoyu)
3 tbsp Sake

Toppings

3 tbs finely chopped Spring Onions (Negi)
1 sheet crumbled dried Seaweed (Nori)
2 tbsp White Sesame Seeds (Shirogomae)
2 tbsp grated Ginger (Shoga)
3 tbsp Mirin
½ cup dried bonito flakes (Katsuoboshi)

1. Combine the dashi, soy sauce, sake, and Mirin in deep saucepan; bring to boil over high heat
2. Add bonito flakes; remove from the heat, strain through cheesecloth-lined strainer
3. Serve warm

Hotpot

1. Fill medium sized saucepan with water; add kombu
2. Heat on medium flame but do not let boil
3. Cut each tofu block into 8 pieces; place in hot stock
4. Simmer 20 minutes
5. Serve ½ cup dipping sauce for each person
6. Serve by individually taking tofu from communal hotpot

Miso Layer Hotpot
(Dotenabe)

½ cup of Red Miso
1 pound of fresh Oysters (Kaki)
6-inch piece of Daikon Radish
3 Chinese Cabbage leaves (Hokusai), cut into 1 ½ inch strips
3 fresh Shiitake Mushrooms
1 Carrot (Ninjin)
6 small Potatoes (Imo)
½ block of grilled (Yaki-dofu)
½ block of Yam Cake (Konnyaku)
3 hardboiled Eggs
1 Leek (Naga Negi)
½ tbsps of Sake
6 cups of Ichiban Dashi

1. Scrub and shell oysters (if not already shelled)
2. Peel potatoes, quarter, parboil; drain and set aside
3. Rehydrate shiitake mushrooms in small bowl of cool water (about 20 minutes)
4. Squeeze excess water out, remove and discard stems
5. Peel daikon radish; cut into rounds ½ inch thick
6. Parboil radish; drain and set aside
7. Peel onion and cut into ¼ inch slices on diagonal
8. Parboil carrot; drain and set aside
9. Wash Leek, cut off root tip (discard); cut into 2-inch lengths on diagonal
10. Parboil konnyaku, drain, cut into 1-inch cubes
11. Cut Tofu into 2-inch cubes
12. Peel hard boiled Eggs, slice, set aside
13. Line inner rim of a medium sized Donabe pot with an inchwide layer of Miso paste
14. Place vegetables into along with the konnyaku, and tofu
15. Add dashi and sake
16. On medium heat, bring Donabe to boil; reduce heat to low
17. Cover and simmer for 30 minutes; Miso will gradually dissolve into broth
18. Serve by placing ingredients in small bowls, ladle some of the hot broth into the bowl, top with a hardboiled egg slice
19. Serve with bowls of hot cooked rice

Shabu-Shabu

1 lb thinly sliced Beef
½ Chinese Cabbage
3 Green Onions
6 Shiitake mushrooms (medium size), stems removed
1 pack of Shirataki Noodles

Broth
6 cupsWwater
7 inch long Konbu (dried kelp)
Sesame Sauce
1 tbsp White Miso
2 tbsp Soy Sauce
1 tbsp konbu dashi (from above)
¼ tbsp Sugar
¼ tbsp Vinegar

*Serve with Rice

Ponzu

*See Ponzu recipe in this section

OPTIONAL: A portable cooktop that can be placed on a table

This is a communal dish cooked in the centre of the table, each person takes as they wish. You will need a large pot , a very deep skillet or a Japanese donabe (clay pot used for hotpot)

SOUP

1. Cut the konbu into 2-3 short pieces and place in a pot with 1L (2.1pt) water; Soak for 30 minutes
2. Bring the water with konbu to a boil over high heat; when small bubbles start rising, remove the konbu. The soup is ready for Shabu-shabu.
3. Cut Chinese cabbage leaves crosswise into 2 inch long pieces
4. Cut green onions diagonally into 5 inch long pieces
5. Rinse Shirataki and drain
6. Plate the vegetables and beef slices on a large serving platter, clustering each ingredient together

Eating

In the centre of the dining table, place the broth in a pot on a portable cooktop with a ladle and a bowl of water next to it.

Place the plate of meat and vegetables near the cooktop and a medium-sized dishes per person with Ponzu in each bowl

1. Bring kombu soup to a boil.
2. Add vegetables to broth.
3. Add a small amount of vegetables of your choice to the broth and cook until tender.
4. Add meat, cooking for about 1 minute
5. Each person takes meat or vegetables as wanted, dipping in Ponzu and eating with rice.
6. When cooking beef slices, foam will surface; Skim foam with ladle occasionally repeating as necessary.

Salmon Miso Hot Pot
(Ishikari Nabe)

6 cups Ichiban Dashi
1 ½ cups Rice
¾ lb Salmon fillet (Sake)
1 block grilled firm Tofu
1 block Yam Cake (Konnyaku)
½ Carrot (Nijin)
4 large leaves Chinese Cabbage (Hokusai)
1 lb Daikon
2/3 cups Miso
2 tbsp Soy Sauce (Shoyu)
2 tbsp Sake
1 tbsp Mirin
4 cups cold, fresh water
1 lb Potatoes
1 tbsp Butter

1. Slice salmon fillet into bite-sized cubes; marinate salmon cubes with soy sauce and mirin
2. Set aside to marinate for 20 minutes
3. Slice Tofu into 2-inch cubes
4. Peel and cut potatoes into 1-inch chunks
5. Wash and peel daikon radish; slice into 1-inch rounds and then into half (like a half-moon)
6. In a medium saucepan, bring daikon radish, rice and water to boil; cook until daikon radish can be pierced with a fork or bamboo skewer
7. Drain and rinse with cold water; set aside
8. Wash and peel carrot; slice into ½-inch pieces on diagonal
9. Boil carrots until tender, drain and set aside
10. Slice devil's tongue into 4" x 2" slices; pour boiling water over them to rinse; set aside
11. Wash Chinese Cabbage and chop into 2-inch pieces
12. In large saucepan or Donabe, bring 4 cups dashi, sake and mirin to boil
13. Add Potatoes and cook until tender
14. Lower heat to medium; add Chinese cabbage, cook until tender
15. Add remaining 2 cups dashi
16. Add Miso, stirring to dissolve miso; add butter
17. Add remaining vegetables
18. Place tofu gently at one side; simmer for 2 minutes
19. Add Salmon, just slightly below the surface of the soup until thoroughly cooked
20. When salmon is cooked, ladle into individual bowls
21. Serve with individual bowls of hot cooked rice

Chicken Stew
(Tori no Mizutaki)

1 lb Chicken Thighs (Tori no Momo)
1 lb medium Tofu, pressed and drained, cut into 1-inch pieces
1 bunch Spinach (Horenso)
1 cup Chinese Cabbage (Hokusai)
2 cups Yam Noodles (Shirataki) or thin Rice Noodles
2 cups Spring Onions (Negi)
1 cup Carrots (Ninjin) thinly Sliced diagonally
6 dried Shiitake Mushrooms, soaked in water (Keep this water.)
1 2x6-inch length dried Kelp (Kombu)
2 tsp Dashi no moto

Dipping Sauce Ponzu:

1/3 cup Soy Sauce (Shoyu)
¼ cup Lemon Juice
1 tbsp Rice Vinegar (Amasu)
1/3 cup Ichiban Dashi

1. Combine soy sauce, lemon juice, rice vinegar and dashi; mix thoroughly and chill
2. Divide equally between 3 dipping sauce dishes
3. Wash chicken in salt water; rinse, pat dry and cut into bite size pieces
4. Soak dried shiitake mushrooms in water for 30 min. to rehydrate; reserve liquid
5. Drain yam noodles; set aside
6. Wash spring onions; trim root ends (discard)
7. Cut spring onions, set aside
8. Peel carrots; chop in ¼ inch chunks on diagonal
9. Wash spinach, remove tough ends (discard) and pat dry
10. Drain tofu if necessary and cut into 2-inch cubes
11. Wash cabbage, chop into 2-inch pieces
12. Add 1 inch of water to a 12-inch table-top skillet (electric or camping stove)
13. Add kombu bring to boil over high heat
14. Remove kombu just before boil
15. Add Dashi no moto and reserved shiitake mushroom water
16. Add chicken, carrots and Chinese cabbage; cook until carrots are tender
17. Add yam noodles, tofu, mushrooms and spinach; cook 2-3 minutes
18. Reduce heat to low simmer
19. When the Nabe is ready, everyone helps themselves
20. Serve with bowls of hot, cooked rice

Sumo Wrestler's Stew
(Chanko Nabe)

6 cups Ichiban Dashi
¼ cup Soy Sauce (Shoyu)
4 tbsp Mirin
¼ lb thinly Sliced sirloin Beef
¼ lb thinly Sliced Pork
¼ lb skinless, boneless Chicken
3 large shrimp (Ebi)
3 scallops (Hotate)
¼ lb fish fillets (eg. Cod, Salmon, Tuna, Mackerel)
3 large Clams or Oysters
3 hard boiled Eggs (Tamago)
1 block Grilled Tofu
3 leaves Chinese Cabbage (Hokusai)
1 Carrot (Ninjin)
1 cup Spinach leaves (Horenso)
3 inchpiece Daikon Radish
¼ cup Bean Sprouts
1 Leek (Naga Negi)
3 medium Potatoes (Imo)
¼ cup dried Seaweed (Wakame)
3 Shiitake Mushrooms
1 block Enoki Mushrooms

Ponzu Dipping Sauce

1/3 cup Soy Sauce (Shoyu)
¼ cup Lemon juice
1 Tbsp Rice Vinegar (Amasu)
1/3 cup Ichiban Dashi
Grated Daikon (Momiji-oroshi)
7-Pepper ix (Shichimi-Togarashi)
¼ Spring onions (Negi)

1. Combine soy sauce, lemon juice, rice vinegar and dashi; mix thoroughly and chill
2. Divide equally between 3 dipping sauce dishes
3. Place grated daikon and spring onions in separate dishes to add to Ponzu
4. Scrub and debeard clams/ shell oysters
5. Shell and de-vein shrimp
6. Salt fish, let sit for 5 minutes; rinse with cold water, pat dry with paper towels
7. Remove bones, skin; cut into bite sized pieces
8. Rinse scallops; pat dry with paper towel
9. Peel potatoes, quarter, parboil; drain and set aside
10. Peel daikon radish; cut into rounds ½-inch thick
11. Parboil radish; drain and set aside
12. Peel onion and cut into ¼-inch slices on diagonal
13. Parboil carrot; drain and set aside
14. Wash leek, cut off root tip (discard); cut into 2-inch lengths on diagonal
15. Wash Chinese cabbage, chop into 2-inch pieces
16. Wash enoki mushrooms; cut off fibery-bottom; separate into small bunches
17. Wash shiitake mushrooms; make criss-cross on tops with knife
18. Rinse chicken with water; cut into bite-sized chunks
19. Rinse spinach leaves; shake out excess water
20. Rinse bean sprouts; remove thread ends
21. Cut tofu in 2-inch cubes
22. Arrange vegetables, fish, and meat on large platter
23. Place camping stove or deep electric skillet in middle of dining table
24. Place Japanese Donabe or deep heat-proof saucepan on camping stove/griddle
25. In Donabe or deep pot, add dashi; bring to boil
26. Reduce heat to medium; start adding some of each of the hard vegetables
27. Add some meat and fish
28. Just before serving, add some tofu, some spinach and some wakame
29. Turn heat to low; add more dashi if needed to keep cooking additional food
30. When the nabe is ready, everyone helps themselves
31. Serve with bowls of hot, cooked rice
32. Udon or thin rice noodles can be added to the leftover dashi if desir

FISH

FISH

Broiled Clams
(Hamaguri no Saka Mushi)

1 lb fresh medium sized Clams or Mussels
1 clove Garlic
1 tbsp Butter
1 tbsp Vegetable Oil
1 tsp Soy Sauce (Shoyu)
1 tsp minced Parsley
1 tbsp Sake or White cooking wine
1 tbsp shaved Lemon peel

1. Wash and clean clams, de-beard mussels, discard broken or opened shellfish
2. Peel and mince garlic finely
3. Heat vegetable oil in skillet or wok on medium heat
4. Add minced garlic and sauté quickly being careful not to brown it
5. Add clams or mussels and stir fry for about 1 minute
6. Add soy sauce and sake; cover to steam 2-3 minutes or until shellfish open
7. Add butter and minced parsley, stir fry until butter melts
8. Sprinkle with grated lemon peel
9. Pour clams and sauce into communal bowl
10. Give each person a small bowl to discard shells in

Easy Salted Salmon
(Shiozake)

6 fresh Salmon steaks (Sake)
2 x ¼ cup Seasalt
1 large plastic freezer-proof zip-lock bags

1. Wash salmon steaks and pat dry with paper towels
2. Remove any visible bones carefully
3. Cut each whole salmon steak in half to make 2 steakettes
4. Place 6 steakettes into each plastic bag
5. Pour ¼ cup seasalt into each bag, remove air from bag and ziplock
6. Massage salt gently around steakettes to make sure each piece is covered
7. Refrigerate 24 hours
8. Remove steakettes, DO NOT RINSE WITH WATER- pat dry with paper towels
9. Leave skin on
10. Wrap 9 steakettes in plastic wrap and freeze for other meals
11. Place 3 steakettes on greased broiler or skillet
12. Fry on each side until slightly brown on each side
13. Remove from heat; place one steakette on each individual plate

Simmered Mackerel
(Saba no Miso Ni)

3 Mackerel fillets
½ cup Sake 1 cup water
1 tbsp Soy Sauce (Shoyu)
2 tbsp Ginger (Shoga)
½ Carrot (Ninjin)
3 inchpiece of Daikon radish
1 bunch Spring onions (Negi)
1 ½ cups sweetened Miso (see recipe below)
3 tsp Seasalt

Sweetened Miso Glaze

1/3 cup White Miso (Shiro Miso)
1/3 cup Country-Style Miso (Inaka Miso)
1 ½ tbsp Sugar (Sato)
1 tbsp Mirin
1 tbsp Sake

1. In small glass bowl, whisk together ingredients; set aside
2. Rub fish with salt; rinse and pat dry with paper towel
3. Peel ginger; finely julienne
4. Peel carrot; julienne into thin, wide strips
5. Peel daikon radish; cut into thin, wide strips
6. Wash spring onions; pat dry with paper towel
7. Slice off root tips (discard); chop finely
8. In wide-bottomed saucepan or skillet, place mackerel skin side up over
9. Cover with ginger and thinly sliced vegetables.
10. Add sake; bring to a quick boil
11. Add water; bring to boil over medium heat
12. Add the soy sauce; return to boil one final time
13. Add sweetened Miso; cover
14. Bring to boil; reduce heat to low; simmer for 10 minutes.
15. Adjust with soy sauce to taste
16. Remove from heat; place one piece of mackerel on each serving dish
17. Cover in vegetables and Miso sauce
18. Garnish with chopped Spring onions

Teriyaki Salmon
(Namazake no Teriyaki)

3 fresh Salmon steaks
1 tbsp Soy Sauce (Shoyu)
1 tbsp Sake

Sauce
3 tbsp Soy Sauce (Shoyu)
3 tbsp Sake
3 tbsp Mirin
1 tbsp Vegetable Oil

1. Place salmon steaks in flat glass dish
2. Mix 1 tbsp soy sauce and 1 tbsp sake; pour over salmon steaks; refrigerate to marinate 20 minutes
3. In small saucepan combine soy sauce, sake and mirin, stir
4. Bring sauce ingredients to boil; remove from heat; set aside
5. Pat salmon steaks dry with paper towel
6. Heat oil in frypan; sauté salmon steaks until lightly brown on underside
7. Turn salmon steaks over; add half of sauce
8. When sauce starts to bubble, turn salmon steaks over again, add remaining sauce
9. When sauce begins to bubble, remove from heat
10. Serve on individual plates, drizzle with cooked sauce from pan

Salted Broiled Horse Makerel
(Sakana no Shio Yaki)

2 x 1lb fresh Horse Mackerel
3 tsp Seasalt
3 metal kebab skewers

1. Clean (gut) fish if not already cleaned (leave skin on)
2. Sprinkle both sides with salt; let stand 30 minutes
3. Using metal skewers, run one skewer through each fish, in & out so that head and tail are up
4. Rub salt on fins and open to "fan" shape
5. Broil both sides taking care not to burn the skin
6. Serve on individual dishes

Baked Flounder
(Ko Garei no Fukusa Mushi)

3 small Flounder
1 tsp Seasalt
1 medium Carrot (Ninjin)
3 dried Shiitake Mushrooms
2 oz Green Beans (Sayaingen)
1 oz Ginger (Shoga)
3 Spring Onion (Negi)
8 tbsp Sake

Plum Soy Sauce
(Ume Shoyu)

2 large Pickled Plums (Umeboshi)
½ tbsp Soy Sauce (Shoyu)
1 tbsp Mirin

2 sheets of foil double the size of each fish

1. Remove seed from umeboshi
2. Push Umeboshi through metal strainer
3. Mix with soy sauce and mirin
4. Clean (gut) flounder if not already cleaned
5. Sprinkle salt on both sides; set aside for 10 minutes
6. Wipe flounder off with paper towel
7. Peel and cut carrot into 1-inch strips
8. Put shiitake mushrooms in warm water to soften; remove stems and slice into strips
9. Remove strings from green beans; julienne into 1 ½ inch lengths
10. Peel ginger; slice into very thin strips
11. Slice spring onion into 1 ½ inch-long pieces; julienne
12. Place each piece of fish on foil; sprinkle 2 tbsp sake on each piece of fish
13. Divide and arrange vegetables among flounder; fold foil to make sealed fish package
14. Bake 20-30 minutes
15. Remove and discard liquid from baking; place fish on individual dishe

Broiled White Fish
(Sawara Yuan Yaki)

6 x 1lb Snapper or other White fish fillets
6 Lime slices
3 tbsp Soy Sauce (Shoyu)
1 ½ tbsp Sake
1 ½ tbsp Mirin
6 large size Bamboo skewers

1. Combine soy sauce, sake, mirin and lime slices in shallow, wide-bottomed dish
2. Add fish fillets, cover, and marinate 15 hours in refrigerator
3. Soak bamboo skewers in water for 30 minutes
4. Thread 1 skewer through each fillet being careful not to pierce the opposite side
5. Broil 7-8 minutes on each side
6. When cooked, remove skewers carefully (twisting the skewers helps) without freaking fish
7. Place 2 fillets on each individual plate, garnish with a fresh lime slice and let cool

Miso-Marinated Broiled Tuna
(Kajiki Maguro Miso Zuke)

1 ½ lb Tuna, fresh or frozen
1 tsp Seasalt
2/3 cup Miso
3 ½ Soy Sauce (Shoyu)
2 tbsp Sake

1. Slice fish fillet in ½-inch thick, 2-inch square pieces
2. Salt each piece evenly; set aside for 5 minutes
3. Combine miso, soy sauce and sake
4. Spread miso mixture on bottom of square glass oven-proof dish
5. Pat tuna pieces dry with paper towel
6. Place tuna pieces in miso mixture; marinate for 12 hours
7. Remove tuna from miso mixture taking off extra miso by hand (DO NOT wash with water)
8. Broil tuna on each side
9. Divide broiled tuna among 3 individual serving dishes

Braised Flounder with Grated Daikon
(Karei no Oroshi Ni)

3 x ½lb Flounder
½ cup Flour
Oil for deep frying

Sauce

1 ½ cups Ichiban Dashi
1 tsp Sugar (Sato)
1 tbsp Mirin
½ tsp Seasalt
1 tbsp Soy Sauce (Shoyu)
1 cup grated Daikon
2 Spring onions (Negi)
1 tbsp grated fresh Ginger (Shoga)

1. Heat oil to 360°F
2. Cut tips off spring onion, discard; slice spring onion thinly
3. Clean and gut flounder if not already done; pat dry with paper towels
4. Cut flounder in half
   *Traditionally, one half retains the head, the other half retains the tail
5. Slice shallow slits on skin
6. Dust with flour
7. Deep fry fish until golden brown, meat next to bone should be cooked
8. Remove with slotted spoon onto paper towel lined baking rack; set aside
9. In medium saucepan, combine Dashi, Mirin, soy sauce and salt; bring to boil
10. Add daikon, onion and grated ginger; stir well
11. In large shallow saucepan, place deep-fried flounder; pour Dashi mixture over fish
12. Simmer 5 minutes
13. Remove fish to large serving platter; cover with remaining simmered sauce
14. Serve hot

Crab and Rice Porridge
(Kani Zosui)

3 cups Ichiban Dashi
2 cups boiled Rice
¼ lb Crab Meat
2 Eggs (Tamago)
¼ cup frozen Green Peas
½ tsp Seasalt
1 tsp Soy Sauce (Shoyu)
1 tbsp Sake
1 Spring Onion (Negi)

1. Wash spring onion; remove tip from spring onion, discard, and mince remainder
2. Separate crab meat pieces
3. Beat eggs; set aside
4. In a large saucepan or nabe, bring dashi to a boil
5. Add seasalt, shoyu and sake; let simmer 5 minutes
6. Add rice and green peas; bring to the boil again
7. Add crab meat; stir mixture and lower to simmer
8. Slowly pour beaten eggs over surface of dashi mixture
9. Cover, remove from heat and let stand until eggs thicken
10. Serve hot in individual bowls

EGGS

EGG DISHES

Steamed Egg Custard (Chawan Mushi)

½ lb boneless, skinless Chicken breast
1 tsp Sake
1 tsp light Soy Sauce (Shoyu)
3 small raw shrimp (Ebi)
3 stalks trefoil (or equivalent amount baby Spinach or Watercress)
3 raw Ginkgo nuts or chestnuts, shelled and peeled

Custard base

3 large Eggs (Tamago)
2 cups Ichiban Dashi
½ tsp Seasalt
1 tbsp Mirin
1 tbsp Soy Sauce (Shoyu)

1. Beat eggs in medium-sized bowl
2. In another bowl, mix the room-temperature dashi, salt, mirin, and light soy sauce
3. Pour mixture in a thin stream into beaten egg; mix well, but do not beat
   The surface of the mixture should be free of foam
4. Drain; set aside
5. Preheat oven to 425°F
6. Cut chicken breast into ½-inch pieces
1. Marinate with 1 tbsp sake and 1 tbsp soy sauce for 15 minutes; drain & discard marinade
2. Blanch shrimp in hot water for 30 seconds, remove, pat dry with paper towels
3. Wash trefoil or other greens, pat dry, and chop coarsely.
4. Shell and peel ginkgo nuts; use whole
5. Peel and slice chestnuts
6. Divide the prepared solid ingredients between 3 oven-proof cups, except for chopped trefoil or greens
7. Ladle the egg stock mixture into the cups, filling to about ½ inch from the top
8. Add chopped greens
9. Cover each cup with foil and set in oven-proof dish
10. Add enough water to cover halfway up the cups; place in oven
11. Bake for 20-30 minutes; insert toothpick into centre to check – toothpick will be clean when finished cooking
12. Serve hot or chilled
    As a custard, it will be slightly jiggly when perfectly cooked

Hot Spring Eggs
(Onsen Tamago)

6 large, fresh Eggs
5 cups water
1 ½ cups Ichiban Dashi
1 tbsp Soy Sauce (Shoyu)

1. Bring eggs to room temperature before cooking
2. In deep saucepan, bring water to boil
3. Remove from heat; add about 3/4 cup of water to pan to bring water temperature to 158-167° F
4. Gently lower eggs into warm water gently; cover the pan
5. Set aside for 25-30 minutes
6. Soak the eggs in cold water
7. In small pan, heat Dashi soup stock and soy sauce
8. Crack eggs into individual small dishes; pour warm Dashi sauce over eggs
9. Serve with bowls of hot, cooked rice

Japanese Soft-Boiled Eggs
(Shoyu Tamago)

6 large, fresh Eggs
3 tbsp White Vinegar
5 cups cold, fresh water

Marinade
1 cup Soy Sauce (Shoyu)
1 cup water
½ cup brown Sugar
1 tbs Mirin
1 knob fresh Ginger

1. Peel ginger and slice into ¼ inch slices (about 10-12 slices)
2. Over medium heat in small saucepan, combine all ingredients; bring to boil
3. Remove from heat; let cool to room temperature
4. Strain liquid through cheesecloth-lined strainer
5. Set aside

1. In deep saucepan, bring 10 cups water and vinegar to boil; turn heat off
2. Add eggs, cover, and let sit 6-7 minutes
3. Using ladle, transfer eggs to rice water immersion bath; let sit for 3 hours
4. Remove shells carefully; set aside
5. In large plastic kitchen bag, pour cooled marinade; add shelled, boiled eggs carefully
6. Zip bag closed, place in refrigerator for 5 hours
7. Bring eggs to room temperature before eating
8. *For ramen topping, slice egg in half and set on noodles with other toppings

Basic Sweet Rolled Eggs
(Tamagoyaki)

4 Eggs (Tamago)
3 Tbsps Ichiban Dashi
2 Tbsp Sugar (Sato)
1 tbsp Sweet Rice Wine (Mirin)
1 tsp Soy Sauce (Shoyu)
½ tsp Vegetable Oil

Beat Eggs in a bowl
Add Dashi and Sugar; mix well
Heat skillet on medium heat
*Preferably, use a square Tamagoyaki pan
Oil pan lightly and evenly

1. Pour ¼ egg mixture in pan and spread over the surface thinly and evenly
2. Cook until half done; fold egg in half toward the bottom side;
3. Oil empty part of pan and pour another ¼ cup of egg mixture in the space and under rolled egg
4. Cook it until half done and roll the egg again, repeating process as folded egg gets thicker, being careful not to brown egg as it cooks
5. Cook the omelet until done
6. Cut tamagoyaki into ½-inch thick pieces

*If you are using a regular skillet, shape tamagoyaki on Bamboo mat

Basic Rolled Eggs
(Dashimaki Tamago)

4 Eggs
¼ cup Ichiban Dashi
½ tbsp Soy Sauce (Shoyu)
½ tbsp Mirin
1 sheet of dried Seaweed (Nori)
1 tsp Vegetable Oil

1. Cut nori into thin strips
2. In medium bowl, break eggs; add dashi, soy sauce, mirin and beat well
3. On medium, heat the square Tamagoyaki pan or round skillet add ¼ tsp vegetable oil; coating pan
4. Pour 1/3 of egg mixture; layer pan completely
5. When surface of the egg is dry around the edges, roll up the omelet upper end of square pan
6. Add ½ tsp vegetable oil on the empty part of the pan
7. Add another 1/3 of egg mixture cover pan completely, lay nori on top
8. When surface of egg is dry, roll omelet, beginning with cooked egg portion
9. Add another 1/3 of egg mixture cover pan completely; add nori strips
10. When surface of egg is dry, roll omelet, beginning with cooked egg portion
11. Remove from heat; place rolled omelet on pan to cool
12. Cut into ¼ slices

Egg Threads
Kinshi Tamago

3 Eggs
1 tsp Sea Salt

1. Break eggs in small bowl; add 1 tsp, sea salt
2. Lightly beat eggs
3. Heat skillet on low heat, coating lightly with oil
4. Pour small amount of egg in pan, coating pan with egg thinly but equally
5. As it cooks thoroughly, turn over the omelet, being careful not to break it
6. Remove from heat; slip omelet onto plate to cool; repeat with remaining egg mixture
7. When omelets are completely cooled, stack on top of each other, roll up and slice thinly like threads; set aside
8. Mix all ingredients for sauce; refrigerate
9. Slice the cucumber and ham thinly into strips
10. Boil Noodles in water for 5 minutes; run under cold water and drain
11. Divide cold, drained noodles among 3 deep bowls
12. Place the cucumber, ham and Kinishi Tamago in groups around the top of the Noodles

Scrambled Eggs with Spinach
Horenso Tamagoyaki

4 Eggs (Tamago)
3 Tbsps Dashi
2 Tbsp Sugar (Sato)
1 tbsp Mirin
1 tsp Soy Sauce (Shoyu)
1 cup Spinach (Horenso)
½ tsp Vegetable Oil for frying

1. Parboil washed Spinach for one minute, stirring so that all the spinach softens
2. Run under cold water for 30 seconds; squeeze out excess water and chop finely
3. Beat the eggs in small bowl; add dashi, mirin, sugar, and soy sauce; mix well
4. Add spinach; mix well.
5. Heat skillet on medium heat
6. *Preferably, use a square Tamagoyaki pan
7. Oil pan lightly and evenly
8. Pour ¼ egg mixture in pan and spread over the surface thinly and evenly
9. Cook until half done; fold egg in half toward the bottom side;
10. Oil empty part of pan and pour another ¼ cup of egg mixture in the space and under the rolled egg
11. Cook it until half done and roll the egg again, repeating process as folded egg gets thicker, being careful not to brown egg as it cooks
12. Cook the omelet until done
13. Let cool; Cut tamagoyaki into ½ inch thick pieces
    *If you are using a regular skillet, shape tamagoyaki on bamboo mat

TOFU DISHES

TOFU

Deep fried Tofu in Broth (AgeDashi Tofu)

3 blocks Japanese silken Tofu
Potato starch/Flour (Katakuriko)
Oil for deep frying

Broth
3 cups Ichiban Dashi
3 tbsp Mirin
3 tbsp Soy Sauce (Shoyu)

Garnish
1 ½ tsp Spring Onions (Negi), finely-chopped
3 tbsp White Radish (Daikon), finely-grated

1. Drain water from tofu; layer sheets of paper
2. towel on a plate, place tofu blocks on top, layer more sheets of paper towel on top of the tofu and place another place on top of this; leave for 20 minutes to remove excess water from the tofu
3. Mix together the broth ingredients; bring to boil and lower heat to simmer; set aside
4. Heat oil to 350°F
5. Cut each block of tofu into 4 large cubes
6. Lightly coat each tofu cube with potato starch/ flour, repeating on each side of cubes evenly
7. Place the flour-coated tofu cubes into oil making sure they do not touch; repeat in batches
8. Fry Tofu cubes for 3-4 minutes until the
9. base is a light golden colour; then gently turning the cubes over until uniformly golden
10. Remove tofu cubes with slotted spoon onto paper towel lined plate to soak up the excess oil
11. Place 4 deep-fried tofu cubes into each bowl; pour broth over tofu.
12. Garnish with ½ tsp chopped spring onion and 1 tsp grated daikon radishes
13. Serve hot

Steamed Tofu Custard
(Kuyamushi)

1 ½ blocks silken Tofu
1 ¾ cup Ichiban Dashi (or Chicken Stock)
¾ cup Spinach (Horenso)
3/4 tbsp Soy Sauce (Shoyu)
3 medium Eggs (Tamago)
3 dried Shiitake Mushrooms
1 ½ tbsp Sake (Japanese Rice Wine)
1 ¼ teaspoon Seasalt (Umi Shio)
3 small oven-proof ramkins

1. Preheat oven to 425° F
2. Beat eggs in medium-sized bowl
3. In another bowl, mix the room-temperature dashi, salt, mirin, and light soy sauce
4. Pour mixture in a thin stream into beaten egg; mix well, but do not beat

**The surface of the mixture should be free of bubbles/ foam (Aku)*

5. Strain; set aside
6. Drain water from tofu; layer sheets of paper towel on a plate, place tofu blocks on top, layer more sheets of paper towel on top of the tofu and place another place on top of this; leave for 20 minutes to remove excess water from the tofu
7. Wash spinach well, remove tough stems
8. Cut into 2-inch lengths
9. Blanch for 1 minute in lightly salted boiling water; drain and run cold water over
10. Squeeze excess water out; divide into 3 equal portions
11. Rehydrate shiitake mushrooms in 1 cup water; drain, squeezing out excess water
12. Remove stems from shiitake; slice thinly into 1/8-inch pieces; set aside
13. Cut tofu into 6 equal squares and put two into each ramekin
14. Divide shiitake mushrooms equally and place in each ramekin
15. Divide spinach equally and place in each ramekin
16. Cover each cup with foil and place in oven-proof dish
17. Add enough water to cover halfway up the cups; place in oven
18. Bake for 20-30 minutes; insert toothpick into centre to check – toothpick will be clean when finished cooking
19. Serve hot

    *As a custard, it will be slightly jiggly when perfectly cooked

Tofu Steak
(Tofu Tsuteki)

3 blocks Soft Tofu
4-5 tbsp Potato Starch (Katakuriko)
2 tbsp grated or finely minced Garlic
1/8 tsp each Seasalt & Pepper
3-4 tbsp Sunflower or Vegetable Oil

Garnish
3 tsp freshly grated Ginger (Shoga)
3 tsp chopped Spring onions (Negi)
3 tsp Bonito fish flakes (Katsuobushi)

Banno Sauce
¼ cup Mirin
¾ cup Soy Sauce (Shoyu)
5-inch piece of dried Kelp (Kombu)

1. Bring mirin to boil in small saucepan; reduce heat to low and cook 2-3 minutes more (to burn off the alcohol)
2. Remove from heat; add soy sauce and kombu
3. Leave to cool for a couple of hours, remove the Kombu refrigerate
4. Peel and grate ginger; finely spring onions.
5. Slice tofu horizontally
6. Drain tofu by placing tofu slabs on paper towel on a plate; cover with paper towel and another plate to remove excess water for 20 minutes
7. Season tofu on both sides with salt and pepper
8. Lightly coat tofu pieces in the potato starch or plain flour
9. Heat 3 tbs oil in skillet; add the tofu, cooking crispy and golden brown; turn over and repeat cooking process
10. Serve with ½ tsp ginger, ½ tsp spring onions and ½ tsp katsuobushi on each slice
11. Drizzle with Banno Sauce

Spicy Tofu
(Marpo Dofu)

3 cups cooked White Rice (Gohan)
½ lb Ground Pork
1 block Medium Tofu
1 clove Garlic (Niniku)
3 - inch knob fresh Ginger (Shoga)
½ Spring Onion (Negi)
1 tbsp Hot Bean Paste (Tobanjan)
3 tbsp Miso
1 tbsp Sake
1 tsp Chicken Stock (Tori Dashi)
1 cup Water
½ tsp Sugar
½ tsp Salt
1 tbsp Potato Starch (Katakuriko)
1 tsp Sesame Oil (Goma Abura)
1 tbsp Vegetable Oil

1. Drain water from tofu; layer sheets of paper towel on a plate, place tofu blocks on top, layer more sheets of paper towel on top of the tofu and place another place on top of this; leave for 20 minutes to remove excess water from the tofu
2. Cut tofu into ½-inch cubes
3. Peel garlic; mince finely
4. Peel ginger; mince finely
5. Wash spring onions, pat dry with paper towel; cut off root tips(discard)
6. Slice spring onions into ¼-inch pieces
7. In medium glass bowl, combine water, miso, sugar, sake, salt, and chicken stock
8. Whisk ingredients together; set aside
9. In wok or skillet on low, heat vegetable oil
10. Stir-fry garlic, ginger, and spring onion with hot bean sprouts paste on low heat for 5 minutes
11. Add ground pork; stir fry over medium heat until cooked
12. Add miso mixture in the wok; bring to a boil
13. Add tofu cubes; simmer on medium heat for 10 minutes
14. Combine starch with 1 tbsp of water; add to wok
15. Add sesame oil; stir gently
16. Remove from heat
17. Add hot rice to individual bowls; pour Marbo Dofu sauce over top
18. Serve hot

Tofu Crab Cakes
(Kani-Tofu Koroke)

2 blocks firm Tofu
1 6 oz can Crab Meat (Kani)
3 dried Shiitake Mushrooms
1 medium Egg (Tamago)
1 tsp Lemon JuRice
6 tbsp Bread Crumbs (Panko)
½ tsp Seasalt (Umi Shio)
1/8 tsp freshly ground Black Pepper
2 tbsp Vegetable Oil

1. Drain water from tofu; layer sheets of paper towel on a plate, place tofu blocks on top, layer more sheets of paper towel on top of the tofu and place another place on top of this; leave for 20 minutes to remove excess water from the tofu
2. Drain canned crab; remove cartilage, break up clumps with fork; set aside
3. Rehydrate shiitake mushrooms in 1 cup water; drain, squeezing out excess water
4. Remove stems from shiitake mushrooms; chop finely into pieces; set aside
5. Beat egg; set aside
6. In medium bowl, crumble or roughly mash tofu
7. Add beaten egg, lemon juice, panko crumbs, salt & pepper; mix well
8. Add chopped shiitake mushrooms and crab meat; mix well
9. Divide mixture into 6 patties
10. Heat oil in skillet over medium heat
11. Gently add 3 patties; fry until golden brown on bottom (5 minutes)
12. Turn patties over; fry bottoms until golden brown
13. Remove to paper towel lined plate; repeat frying process for final 3 crab cakes
14. Serve hot with lemon slices or tartar sauce

Chicken Tofu Patties
(Tori Tofu Koroke)

1 lb firm Tofu
3/4 lb Ground Chicken
3/4 cup Panko (breadcrumbs) (Panko)
1 medium Egg
¼ cup Spring Onion
1 - inch knob fresh Ginger, peeled and grated
2 tsp Seasalt (Umi Shio)
Oil for frying

Sauce

4 Tbsp soy sauce
3 Tbsp Mirin
2 tbsp water
Prepare as patties are cooking
Combine ingredients in small saucepan, bring to boil

Garnish

3 tsp grated Daikon radish

1. Drain water from tofu; layer sheets of paper towel on a plate, place tofu blocks on top, layer more sheets of paper towel on top of the tofu and place another place on top of this; leave for 20 minutes to remove excess water from the tofu
2. Peel and grate ginger
3. Wash spring onions, pat dry with paper towel; cut off root tips (discard)
4. Chop spring onions finely
5. In medium bowl mash tofu with fork
6. Add egg, ginger, green onion, panko crumbs, salt and chicken; mix well
7. Divide into 3 patties
8. Heat oil in skillet over medium heat.
9. Fry until golden brown (appr. 5 minutes)
10. Gently turn patties over and cover skillet; reduce heat
11. Cook on low heat for a few minutes until cooked
12. Remove patties with slotted spatula to paper towel lined plate
13. Place patties on individual plates
14. Top patties with grated daikon radish; pour the sauce over
15. Serve hot

Anchovy Peanut Tofu
(Jakopi Tofu)

3 blocks of Soft Tofu
¼ cup dried anchovies (Chirimenjako)
¼ cup Peanuts or cashews
1 bunch Spring Onions (Negi)
1 tbsp Sesame Seeds (Goma)
2 tsp Sesame Oil (Goma Abura)

1. Drain water from tofu; layer sheets of paper towel on a plate, place tofu blocks on top, layer more sheets of paper towel on top of the tofu and place another place on top of this; leave for 20 minutes to remove excess water from the tofu
2. Place 1 block tofu on each plate
3. Wash spring onions, pat dry with paper towel; cut off root tips (discard)
4. Chop spring onions finely
5. Chop peanuts or cashews roughly
6. In skillet, heat sesame oil over medium
7. Add nuts and Chirimenjako; stir fry 2 minutes
8. Add the spring onions and sesame seeds; stir fry 2 minutes
9. Remove from heat
10. Top tofu with Jakopi; drizzle with soy sauce per taste
11. Serve hot

Okara and Vegetable Sauté
(Unohana no Iri Ni)

2 Tbsps oil, half Sesame Oil and half Vegetable Oil
1 small Carrot
1 Spring Onion (Negi)
10 dried Shiitake Mushrooms
1 cup Okara, packed tightly
1 cup Ichban Dashi
2 to 3 tbsp honey
2 tbsp Soy Sauce (Shoyu)
1 tbsp Sake

1. Rehydrate shiitake mushrooms in 1 cup water; drain, squeezing out excess water
2. Remove stems from shiitake mushrooms; slice thinly into 1/8-inch pieces; set aside
3. Peel carrot and julienne into matchsticks; set aside
4. Wash spring onions, pat dry with paper towel; remove root tips (discard)
5. Julienne spring onions; set aside
6. In a skillet heat oils over medium
7. Add julienned carrots; sauté 2 minutes
8. Add julienned onions; sauté until transparent
9. Add sliced shiitake mushrooms; sauté 1 minute
10. Add remaining ingredients; bring mixture to boil
11. Reduce heat; simmer for 15 minutes (stirring occasionally) until liquid has absorbed/evaporated
12. Remove from heat; cool to room temperature
13. Serve as side dish

Simple Cold Tofu
(Hiyakko Tofu)

3 blocks Silken Tofu
3 tbsp dried Bonito fish flakes (Katsuobushi)
3 tsp Spring Onion (Negi)
3 tsp grated Ginger
3 tbsp Soy Sauce (Shoyu)

1. Wash, dry and chop spring onion
2. Drain tofu, pat dry with paper towel and place on individual plates
3. Top tofu with grated ginger, dried bonito flakes, and chopped green onion
4. Pour approximately 1 tbsp soy sauce over each tofu block before eating
5. Serve chilled

Tofu Fritters
(Ganmodoki)

1 block firm Tofu
10 dried Shiitake Mushrooms
1 Carrot (Ninjin)
2 tbsp Spring Onion (Negi)
3 tbsp grated Potato (Imo)
1 Egg White
1 tsp Seasalt (Umi Shio)
1 tbsp Corn or Potato starch
1 tbsp cooked sea grass (Hijiki)

Dipping Sauce

3 tbsp Soy Sauce (Shoyu)
Japanese mustard (Karashi)

1. Drain water from tofu; layer sheets of paper towel on a plate, place tofu blocks on top, layer more sheets of paper towel on top of the tofu and place another place on top of this; leave for 20 minutes to remove excess water from the tofu
2. Rehydrate shiitake mushrooms in 1
3. cup water; drain, squeezing out excess water
4. Remove stems from shiitake mushrooms; slice thinly into 1/8-inch pieces; set aside
5. Peel carrot and julienne into matchsticks; blanch in boiling water (appr. a minute)
6. Drain blanched carrots; set aside
7. Blanche seagrass in boiling water for 2 minutes
8. Drain seagrass and set aside
9. Wash spring onions, pat dry with paper towel; remove root tips(discard)
10. In medium bowl, mash tofu with a fork
11. Add all ingredients mixing well
12. Heat oil to about 320°F
13. Form tofu mixture into small patties
14. Deep fry 2-3 at a time
15. Remove from oil with slotted spoon to paper towel lined plate
16. Serve immediately with soy sauce and mustard (Karashi Jo-yu)

NOODLES

NOODLE DISHES

Standard noodle cooking instructions

For cooking Soba (buckwheat), or Udon (White Flour) Noodles, you'll need a deep pot and a colander.

Fill the pot half-way with water and bring to a rolling boil.

*Be sure to place the noodles in the pot only when the water is extremely hot

- Stir occasionally to make sure the noodles don't stick to each other, adding ¼ cup cold water to the pot when it threatens to boil over; repeat this 2 more times
- Have hot water running in your sink and place the colander in the basin
- Pour the pot of boiling noodles into the colander and allow hot water to run over the strainer full of noodles until the water runs clear

*If improperly washed the noodles will be starchy and sticky
Allow Noodles to drain; serve with hot dipping sauce or in soup

*To make noodles to be served cold, after boiling rinse noodles in cold water until the water runs clear; place in ice water for a few minutes, rinse again, drain and serve with cold dipping sauce

Treasure-Chest Udon
Nabeyaki Udon

2/3 lb. dried Udon Noodles or 3 packages fresh Udon

6 cups Ichiban Dashi

6 tbsp Soy Sauce (Shoyu)

3 tbsp Mirin

1 tsp Seasalt (Umi Shio)

½ lb. Chicken Thighs (Tori no Momo)

3 fresh Shiitake Mushrooms

1 bunch Spinach (Horenso)

3 Spring Onion (Negi)

½ Carrot (Ninjin)

3 Eggs (Tamago)

1. Wash chicken in salted water, drain and chop into 2-inch chunks
2. Wash shiitake mushrooms, detach stems (discard)
3. Make criss-cross on top of each mushroom cap; set aside
4. Wash spring onions; cut off ends and discard
5. Cut spring onions ½-inch below where the green grows from the whites; set aside
6. Wash and parboil spinach in boiling water with pinch of salt
7. Drain and rinse with cold water and drain again; squeeze out excess water
8. Cut pressed Spinach into 1-inch lengths
9. Peel Carrot and slice into ¼-inch rounds
10. Boil water in large kettle
11. Add udon noodles and cook for 8-10 minutes (less for fresh udon)
12. When the water begins to boil over, add 1 cup of cold water and wait for the next boil
13. Remove from heat, drain and rinse well in cold water; drain again, set aside
14. Heat dashi stock; add soy sauce, salt, mirin and bring to boil
15. Prepare individual heat-proof casserole bowls or Donabe bowl
16. Divide noodles and place noodles in each dish
17. Divide chicken and vegetables evenly on noodles
18. Pour Dashi stock in until ½-inch from top of each dish
19. Cover and cook on high heat until boiling
20. Break 1 egg into each dish; cover and cook 1 to 2 minutes or until cooked

Cold Soba Noodles and Dipping Sauce
(Zaru Soba)

1 ten-once package of dried Soba Noodles

Dipping Sauce
1 ¼ cups of Ichiban Dashi
½ cup of Soy Sauce (Shoyu)
¼ cup Mirin
1 teaspoon Sugar *OR* Bottled Mentsuyu or Memmi prepared to label instructions

Toppings
1 sheet dried seaweed paper (Nori) sheets
½ block of chilled Tofu cut into small 1-inch cubes
4 tbsps of finely Diced Spring onions (Negi)
1 tbsp of Wasabi

1. Mix and heat the dipping sauce ingredients in a small saucepan, remove and refrigerate
2. Toast nori by holding nori 6-8 inches over low heat, turning over side-to-side for 1 minute, toasting the nori on both sides; cool and crumble or shred
3. Prepare dried soba noodles using basic noodle cooking instructions for cold noodles (rinse well in a colander using cold water, drain, then place in rice water, drain again)
4. Serve the soba on a woven bamboo tray (Zaru) or small lacquer bowls
5. Place the cubed tofu on top, and garnish

Cold Chinese Noodles
(Hiyashi Chukka Ramen)

3 packages uncooked Chinese Ramen Noodles (Nama Chukka Ramen)
1 Seedless Cucumber or Japanese Cucumber (Kyuri)
6 slices Cooked Ham
1 Tomato
1 tsp Sugar (Sato)
Kinishi Tamago (see recipe in "Eggs")

Sauce
6 tbsp Soy Sauce (Shoyu) 4 tbsp Sugar (Sato)
6 tbsp Rice Vinegar (Amasu)
1 tbsp Sesame oil (Goma Abura)
1 tbsp White Sesame Seeds (Gomae)
Japanese Karashi (optional)

13. Sprinkle with sesame seeds
14. Pour chilled sauce over noodles
15. Serve chilled

Full-Moon Soba
(Tsukimi Soba)

1 package dried Soba (buckwheat Noodles)

Soup
6 cups Ichiban Dashi
1/3 cup Soy Sauce (Shoyu)
2 tbsps Mirin
½ tsp Seasalt (Umi Shio) OR bottled Mentsuyu or Memmi prepared to label instructions
3 Eggs
2 tbsps finely chopped Spring Onion (Negi)
7 Pepper mix (Shichimi)

1. Cook noodles as to basic noodle cooking instructions
2. In large saucepan, heat dashi, soy sauce, mirin, and salt
3. Divide soba noodles into four bowls
4. Pour hot soup over soba noodles
5. Crack one egg on top of noodles in each bowl
6. Sprinkle spring onion and Shichimi on top of noodles

Tempura with Noodles
(Kakiage Soba)

1/3 cup Soy Sauce (Shoyu)
2 tbsps Mirin
½ tsp Seasalt
7 Pepper mix (Shichimi)
Prepare Tempura
Prepare Soba to basic noodle cooking instructions
6 cups Ichiban Dashi OR Bottled Mentsuyu prepared to label instructions

1. In large saucepan, heat dashi, soy sauce, mirin, and salt
2. Divide soba noodles into four bowls
3. Pour hot soup over soba noodles
4. Place several pieces of tempura vegetables and shrimp on each bowl
5. Sprinkle with Shichimi as desired

Hot Noodles and Chicken in Broth (Tori Nanban)

14-ounce package dried wide Udon Noodles (Futonage Udon)
5 ½ tsps Seasalt
½ pound skinless, boneless Chicken Breast or Thighs
3 cups Ichiban Dashi
3 tbsp Soy Sauce (Shoyu)
3 Spring onions (Negi), including at least 3 inches of the green stems

1. Cut spring onions in half lengthwise, continue to slice thinly
2. Bring 2 quarts of water to a boil in large saucepan
3. Drop in the noodles, return to a boil and, stirring occasionally, cook uncovered for about 20 minutes, until the noodles are very soft
4. Stir in 1 tbsp of the salt, cover the pan tightly, and turn off the heat; allow noodles to rest covered for 5 minutes
5. Drain; set aside
6. Cut each boned chicken breast in half horizontally, then into strips about ¼ inchwide by 2 -- inches long
7. In medium saucepan, combine the dashi, sugar, remaining 2 ½ teaspoons of salt and soy sauce; stir and bring to a boil, uncovered
8. Add the noodles, return to a boil, and remove from the heat
9. Using slotted spoon, remove the noodles from the soup and divide them among 3 deep bowls
10. Drop strips of chicken and the spring onions into soup
11. Bring soup to a boil again over high heat, boil for 2 minutes
12. Divide contents of the pan over noodles
13. Serve immediately

Pan-fried Ramen Noodles (Yakisoba)

1 (1lb) package Fresh Chinese Ramen Noodles (Nama Chukkamen)
¼ lb. Boneless Pork Ribs, thinly sliced
¼ cup peeled (Ninjin)
1 Green Bell Pepper, chopped (Piman)
¼ medium Onion (Tamanegi)
3 leaves green head Cabbage (Kabbaji), shredded
4-6 Tbsps. Yakisoba sauce (or premade - bottled or powdered)
½ Tbsp Vegetable Oil

Garnish

Pickled Ginger (Beni Shoga) Dried Seaweed flakes (Aonori) Salt and Pepper

Yakisoba Sauce

¼ cup Soy Sauce (Shoyu)
2 tbsp Worcestershire sauce
1½ tbs Rice Vinegar
1 tbs Sake
1 tbs Mirin
3 tbs Tomato Sauce
1 tbs Oyster Sauce
1 tsp soft Brown Sugar
Shichimi Chili Pepper to taste
Ginger to taste

1. Peel carrots; julienne
2. Wash cabbage leaves; shredded
3. Wash green pepper; halve & seed
4. Slice green pepper thinly
5. Peel onion; slice thinly
6. Combine all ingredients in small saucepan
7. Heat over low for 15 minutes, stirring frequently; remove from heat and cool
8. Lightly loosen uncooked/raw noodles and set aside
9. Heat vegetable oil in medium skillet on medium heat
10. Stir-fry the pork until almost cooked
11. Sprinkle with salt and pepper to season
12. Add carrots, onion, and green bell pepper in the skillet; stir-fry
13. Add cabbage to skillet
14. Add noodles to skillet, pour ¼ cup of water over the noodles and cover
15. Lower heat; steam for 3-5 minutes
16. Remove the lid; add Yakisoba sauce;
17. Stir fry noodles quickly making sure sauce is evenly distributed
18. Transfer to communal plate
19. Sprinkle with seaweed flakes and pickled ginger

Soy Sauce & Butter Ramen (Shoyu-Battah Ramen)

3 servings Fresh Chinese Noodles (Nama Chukkamen) (or 3 packages of dried Ramen Noodles)
3 cloves grated fresh Garlic (Niniku)
3 tsp grated fresh Ginger (Shoga)
3 tsp Sesame Oil (Goma Abura)
3 cups Chicken soup stock
3 cups Kombu Dashi
3 tbsp Sake
½ tsp Seasalt
3 tsp Sugar
¼ cup Soy Sauce
3 tsp Butter

Garnish

Chopped Spring Onion (Negi)
Shredded dried Seaweed (Nori) 7
7-Pepper mix (Shichimi)

Soup Base

1. Heat sesame oil over medium heat in deep saucepan; sauté ginger and garlic
2. Lower heat
3. Add chicken soup stock and kombu dashi soup stock to pan and bring to boil
4. Add sugar, salt, sake, and soy sauce; bring to boil
5. Remove from heat; strain soup through cheesecloth-lined strainer
6. Pour hot soup into 3 deep individual noodle bowls; top each with 1 tsp Butter

Noodles

1. In large saucepan, bring 10 cups water to rolling boil
2. Add Chukkamen noodles to boiling water and cook 3-5 minutes
3. Drain the Noodles, divide amongst bowls and cover with hot soup
4. Garnish with chopped spring onion, shredded seaweed and a dash of 7-Pepper mix

Corn Butter Ramen
(Kohn-Butta Ramen)

3 servings fresh Chinese Noodles (Nama Chukkamen) (or 3 packages of dried Ramen Noodles)
6 cups Chicken Broth
1 clove grated Garlic (Niniku)
½ cup Butter
¼ cup Soy Sauce (Shoyu)
2 cups Corn Kernels, fresh or frozen
1 cup fresh Bean Sprouts (Moyashi)
1 cup canned Sliced Bamboo Shoots, drained
3 tbsp toasted Sesame Seeds

Soup Base

1. Peel garlic and grate
2. Wash and pat dry bean sprouts
3. Pour chicken broth into medium stock pan; bring to boil
4. Add soy sauce, stir, and lower heat to simmer
5. In skillet, melt Butter over medium heat; add grated garlic; stir fry 30 seconds
6. Add corn kernels; gently stir fry until tender crisp
7. Add bean sprouts stir frying constantly for about 30 seconds
8. Add drained, sliced bamboo shoots, stir fry constantly for 1 minute
9. Remove from heat; set aside
10. Place cooked Chukkamen noodles into serving bowls.
11. Top with corn mixture
12. Sprinkle with toasted sesame seeds
13. Add an additional pat of butter to each bowl

Noodles

1. In large saucepan, bring 10 cups water to rolling boil
2. Add Chukkamen noodles to boiling water and cook 3-5 minutes
3. Drain the noodles, divide amongst bowls, and cover with hot soup
4. Divide topping mixture equally among bowls and serve

Miso Ramen

3 servings fresh Chinese Noodles (Nama Chukkamen)(or 3 packages of dried Ramen Noodles)
6 cups Ichiban Dashi
2 tsp Vegetable Oil
1 6-inch strip dried Kelp (Kombu)
3 tsp Soy Sauce (Shoyu)
3 tsp Sugar (Sato)
¼ cup White Miso paste (Shiro Miso)
1 tbsp Sake
2 cloves grated fresh Garlic (Niniku)
1 tbsp fresh grated Ginger (Shoga)
3 tsp Sesame Oil (Goma-Abura)

Garnish

Washed Bean Sprouts (Moyashi)
Sliced Spring onions (Negi)
Julienned Daikon radish, squeezed/ drained
Canned Bamboo shoots
Sliced cooked pork

Soup Base

1. In deep saucepan, bring Dashi, soy sauce, sugar, kombu, garlic, and ginger to a boil
2. Lower heat; simmer 20 minutes; remove kombu (discard)
3. Add sake; add miso paste and stir until dissolved
4. Add sesame oil and stir; continue to simmer on low

Noodles

1. In large saucepan, bring 10 cups water to rolling boil
2. Add Chukkamen Noodles to boiling water and cook 3-5 minutes
3. Drain the Noodles, divide amongst bowls and cover with hot soup
4. Divide topping mixture equally among bowls and serve

Ramen Burger

1 package instant ramen noodles
2 tbsps vegetable oil
¼ lb freshly ground beef, formed into two 4-ounce patties
2 slices American, Cheddar, or Swiss cheese
Kosher salt and freshly ground black pepper
  Other toppings as desired

1. Cook noodles according to package directions, draining 1 minute before time indicated on package; Transfer to a rimmed baking sheet and spread out to allow them to dry slightly. Season to taste with salt and pepper
2. Divide noodles into 6 piles
3. Heat oil in a large non-stick or cast-iron skillet over medium-high heat until shimmering. Place ring mold or empty 28-ounce can with both ends cut off on one side of pan
4. Place 1 pile of noodles into mold and press down gently with a rubber spatula to form a thin, even layer.
5. Carefully lift mold. Repeat with other piles of noodles until you have four circular piles of noodles cooking. Cook until well browned on first side, about 3 minutes
6. Carefully flip and brown on second side, about 3 minutes longer; Transfer to a plate and set aside
7. Season meat with ramen seasoning packet, adding additional salt and pepper to taste
8. Wipe out skillet with paper towel and heat over high heat until lightly smoking
9. Add burger patties and press down immediately with a stiff spatula so that patties are flattened and contact with skillet
10. Cook until seared on first side, about 2 minutes
11. Carefully scrape up patties and flip over
12. Top with cheese and continue to cook until desired doneness is achieved
13. Top bottom ramen buns as desired, add burger patties, top with second ramen buns, and serve immediately

DESSERT

DESSERTS

Japanese Strawberry Shortcake

2 Egg yolks
4 Egg Whites
½ cup plus
2 tbsps Sugar
7 tbsps milk
3 tbsps melted Butter
¾ cup plus 1 tbsp all-purpose Flour
1 teaspoon baking powder
1 teaspoon vanilla extract
1 teaspoon Lemon zest (optional)
Pinch of Salt
Strawberries for filling
Whipped cream

1. Whisk egg whites and lemon zest.
2. Once they start to foam, gradually add the sugar in to form the meringue.
3. Once meringue has stiff peaks, set it aside.
4. In a separate bowl, beat egg yolk and vanilla extract before adding in milk and melted butter; Mix well
5. Stir in flour until dough has a uniform consistency and colour.
6. Add a few tbsps of meringue into the mixture before adding the rest of the mixture into meringue.
7. Pour batter into 2 pans lined with butter and parchment paper; spread out evenly with a spatula.
8. Bake the cakes in a preheated oven at 325°F
9. between 20-25 minutes.
10. Allow cakes to cool for 5 minutes before removing them from the tray to cool completely.
11. Coat the cake with a layer of whipped cream evenly before topping it with thinly-Sliced strawberries.
12. Repeat layering and top with second layer of cake
13. Complete top layer with whipped cream.
14. Slice off sides of the cake to reveal the strawberries and layers.
15. Garnishing with strawberries.

Japanese Parfait

1 ¾ cups heavy cream
3 tbsp Sugar
- Strawberries
- Canned yellow peach
- Apple
- Honeydew melon
- Banana
- Kiwi
- Orange
- Cherries

1/ cup Corn flakes or Granola
3 cups Ice cream of any flavour
3 slices Sponge cake

1. Whip heavy cream and Sugar to form soft peaks. Keep refrigerated until needed.
2. Cut strawberries and peaches into very small pieces.

*Set aside a few whole strawberries for garnishing.

3. Tear sponge cake into 1-inch squares.
4. Cut the rest of the fruit into bite pieces
5. In a parfait glass or Rice cream dish, layer chopped strawberries, Corn flakes, ice cream, peaches, and sponge cake pieces topping each layer with whipped cream
6. Top parfait off with a scoop of ice cream.
7. Garnish dessert with fruits around the Rice cream.
8. Top with whipped cream and a cherry on top of the Rice cream.

Mochi

1 cup Mochiko (Rice Flour)
2 cups Sugar
¾ cup water
Cornstarch for dusting the dough

1. Mix the flour and water together until it reaches a soft dough-like consistency
2. Slowly add more water if needed
3. Steam Mochi for about 20 minutes
4. Transfer Mochi to a pot.
5. Over low to medium heat, add a third of the Sugar and mix into Mochi until completely dissolved.
6. Add another third and repeat until all Sugar has dissolved into Mochi.

*The sugar is key to keeping the Mochi soft and chewy. You can reduce the amount of sugar if you are going to serve it right away.)

7. Once the Mochiko is soft, sticky, and shiny, transfer to a tray sprinkled with cornstarch.
8. Dust hands with some cornstarch to help prevent burning hands.
9. Carefully shape Mochi into balls and serve.

Japanese Cheesecake

½ cup Butter
½ cup Cream Cheese
¾ cup Milk
8 Egg Yolks
¼ cup Flour
¼ cup Cornstarch
13 large Egg Whites
¾ cup Sugar

1. Mix butter, cream cheese, and milk into a pot and cook over low heat stirring until thickened
2. Whisk the egg yolks together in a bowl and gradually whisk in the mixture.
3. Sift the flour and cornstarch over the batter and stir until it's smooth and shiny.
4. In a separate bowl, whisk the egg whites together until soft peaks form.
5. Gradually pouring the sugar in 3 parts to ensure that all the sugar is dissolved into the meringue, add sugar to form a meringue with somewhat-stiff peaks.
6. Gradually fold meringue into batter in small batches stirring gently to keep air inside the mixture
7. Transfer mixture into a round greased baking pan lined with parchment paper. Tap pan gently on counter to remove any air bubbles
8. Place baking pan over a wider baking dish and fill outer tray with 1 inch hot water
9. Bake cheesecake in a preheated oven for 25 minutes at 325°F
10. Reduce heat to 275°F and bake for another 55 minutes.
11. Once cheesecake is baked, carefully invert the cake onto a plate, this will
12. Serve the cake with a layer of powdered Sugar and freshly Sliced fruits of your choice.

Mitarashi Dango

Dango (Rice Flour Balls)

½ cup Shiratamako (lumpy glutinous Rice Flour)
1 block Kinugoshi-Tofu (silken Tofu)
1 teaspoon Sugar (Sato)

1. Mix the ingredients together and knead to form a dough
2. Adjust the texture by adding more Shiratamako or water, until the texture of the dough is like your earlobe
3. Divide the dough into 12 parts
4. Roll each part of the dough into a 2 inchball
5. Drop Dango into a pot of boiling water
6. *The Dango will float after a minute or so. After it begins to float, let it boil for another minute
7. Remove Dango from boiling water and submerge into cold water for one minute; drain well
8. Put 3 to 5 Dango on to each skewer
9. Pan-fry Dango until sides are slightly golden

Mitarashi Sauce

3 tbsps water
1 tbsp Soy Sauce
1 tbsp Sugar
½ tbsp Katakuriko (Potato starch)
Anko (Red Bean paste)

1. Mix the ingredients together in a pot.
2. Cook over low heat, stirring constantly until sauce thickens to a syrupy consistency.
3. For extra sweetness, add 2 tbsp of mirin
4. Brush the Mitarashi sauce onto the Dango balls and top with Anko red bean paste.

Japanese Coffee Jelly

1 tbsp Gelatin Powder
4 tbsp Water
2 cups Coffee
2 tbsp Sugar
Whipped Cream

1. Combine gelatin powder and 4 tbsps of water
2. Place coffee and sugar in saucepan; bring to near boil over medium-high heat
3. Turn off heat, whisking in gelatin mix until it dissolves.
4. Cool and pour into shallow baking dish and refrigerate 5 hours
5. Once coffee jelly has set, cut gelatin into ½-inch cubes
6. Spoon cubes into individual serving dishes, topping with whipped cream, if desired

Castella Cake

4 Medium sized Eggs (room temperature)
½ cup White Sugar
2-3 tbsps Honey
½ cup All Purpose Flour

1. Preheat oven to 350°F
2. Using a double boiler, beat eggs and sugar over simmering boiling water high speed for 6 minutes quadrupling volume of the beaten eggs.
3. Turning beater to medium speed, add honey into egg mixture and beat for 30 seconds.
4. Continuing at medium speed, slowly add into mixture by ¼ cups beating final addition for 1 minute taking care not to overmix.
5. Pour batter into parchment paper lined baking tin
6. Using a Bamboo or wooden skewer, slowly draw zigzag line to remove any air bubbles from the batter for evenly textured cake.
7. Bake for 10-15 minutes until the top turns a rich brown.
8. Cover it with cooking foil; lower the temperature to 340°F and continue baking for another 30-34 minutes. Skewer poke will come out clean the cake is done.
9. When cake is done, remove from tin and immediately cover with plastic wrap/ cling film.

No-Bake Green Tea Mousse Cheesecake

1 (4.8 ounce) package Graham Crackers, crushed
2 tbsp White Sugar
3 tbsp Unsalted Butter, melted
2 tbsp green tea powder (matcha)
½ cup warm water
2 tbsp unflavored gelatin
½ cup cold water
2 cups whipping cream
2 (8 ounce) packages cream cheese, at room temperature
½ cup white sugar
1 teaspoon vanilla extract
¼ cup honey
2 eggs

1. Combine the graham cracker crumbs with 2 tbsps of sugar in a mixing bowl.
2. Drizzle in the melted butter and mix until evenly moistened.
3. Press into the bottom of a 9-inch springform pan lined with waxed paper; set aside.
4. Stir the tea powder into the warm water; set aside. Sprinkle the gelatin over the cold water; set aside.
5. Whip the cream to stiff peaks; set aside.
6. Beat the cream cheese, ½ cup sugar, vanilla, and honey in a clean mixing bowl.
7. Beat in the eggs one at a time until evenly blended.
8. Cook the gelatin mixture in the microwave until melted, about 45 seconds.
9. Beat the gelatin and tea into the cream cheese mixture; fold in the whipped cream until smooth.
10. Pour into the springform pan.
11. Chill overnight before unmolding and serving.

How to Plan a Japanese Meal

Traditionally, typical Japanese meal will have miso soup and rice (with as many refills as you like), pickles, one main meat or fish dish and two or three side dishes. Sushi is generally served with miso soup and pickles on the side. Mix & match your favourites and have fun!

Using Leftovers - How to Make a Bento Lunch Box

The term "bento" roughly translates to "box lunch" in English, this is not your average packed lunch. The goal with bento is to create a well-balanced meal that is just as appealing to the eyes as it is to the taste buds, and it's a fantastic way to use left-overs! Choose colorful foods for visual impact. Make things fun like cutting sandwiches and fruits into shapes using cookie-cutters and putting different textures beside each other.

- Buy a traditional bento box with sectioned compartments from Amazon or your favourite dollar store.

- Start by dividing the food proportionally, then place each food in a separate compartment of your bento box. Aim for a variety of colors, flavors, and textures for an authentic experience. Mix & match your favourites and have fun!

- Rice or another carbohydrate should make up 50% of the meal.
  Tip: Try flavoring the rice by using the recipes from Japanese Cooking for Gaijin or small pre-made packets which come in a variety of flavors and can be purchased at Asian markets.

- A protein to make up 25% of the meal. Protein serves as a filling side portion and should make up about ¼ of the bento box. More traditional bento boxes may include salmon, tuna, or whitefish, but other lean meats, hard-boiled eggs, or cheeses can be substituted – it's your lunch box, use what you love! It's traditional to use 2 different proteins, but you don't have to.

YOUR DARUMA FOR SUCCESS - MAKE A WISH!

Write your intention or wish and colour in one eye with a black marker. When your wish comes true, colour in the other eye!

NOTES

海千山千

NOTES

海千山千

www.ingramcontent.com/pod-product-compliance
Lightning Source LLC
Chambersburg PA
CBHW051256110526
44589CB00025B/2852